Politics
As

Usual

Run for Something or Fall for Anything

Erick Wright

Introduction:

The purpose of compiling a book was not for fortune, fame, or glory. Praise doesn't mean anything to me in this point and junction in my life. This book does not mean that I am a political guru nor does it mean my political experience is the only way of thinking. There is no invisible Geppetto pulling, tugging, or twisting my strings. I am not a wealthy man; not a rich or well-to-do. I'm not a genius nor am I perfect by any stretch of the imagination. I have only one notable trait that I possess, one that is often overlooked and unaccounted for. It cannot be purchased at a convenience store, not even with the fortune of Donald Trump, the Koch brothers, and Oprah combined. It was given to me by the Almighty. I have heart!

Such a trait will pick a boxer up from the canvas to rise to victory. It gives a soldier the strength to charge back into the battlefield for a wounded brother-in-arms. It is from the heart that this message is given to you.

This book is not to make you change your beliefs or force you against your faith. This book is not written to bash the state of Alabama, its history, or future. This book is not written to convince you nor convert you to a political ideology. Although I am an indigenous American/Black American, this book will not play the race card. There will be no exploitation of race relations or atmosphere in Alabama. Furthermore, neither will the love for Christianity or any other religion be forced on you. I'm descendent of over a 1,000 years (via the Arab and transatlantic slave trade) of such atrocities. I do not intend on committing the same crime. You are capable of coming to your own conclusion regarding the information that is presented.

Now that we fully understand what this text is not, I will give you my reasoning for putting together this body of work. I will try to explain something with no explanation to give guide were there are no paths. The thing that allows children to starve and be homeless, the thing that preys on young black males for slave labor, the thing that allows your food to contain the very ingredients that gives you the diseases scientists are so rabidly searching for a cure, the thing that allows the police department to have a tank, but leads the nation in murders of unarmed men, the thing that over taxes the poor, the vicious thing that told you going college means a better life, the reason your friends and family keep dying in war, the reason you learn incorrect history in school, the reason why we still idiotically attend school on a farmers calendar, the reason your power company hasn't upgraded or replaced the 30-year-old power lines and street lights, the reason why you can't find full time work, the reason temp work is a gimmick by not offering benefits, the reason you can't unionize. All of the reasons for writing this book. What's reason…what's the answer? Politics!

Yes, politics is one of the most persistent driving factors of our existence. In addition, the idea or notion that American politics is designed for the rich, elite, or children of former politicians and aristocrats should set a fire in your soul. Politics is seen to be the holy grail of all professions in America; this is obvious by the lack of accountability. Also, the profession has had little to no change and probably has arguably the lowest turnover rate of employees in the last 50 years. To the citizens, the normal Joes, and everyday workers, this profession is normally out of reach for most. Because of this fact we are unwilling to enter into the proverbial lion's den of public service.

I was among the millions of artificial second-class citizens that subscribe to this way of thinking. In this world we are less likely to publicly voice our opinions because we feel inferior. Inaction can due to a job or a position that does not allow us to speak what our heart believes without fear of reprisal. This is especially true in the Indigenous Black community we are the most afraid.

Why be afraid of politics? Just maybe the stories of our past and events in history have subconsciously stuck with us. Seeing time and time again brave souls that raise voices and stand when others don't, they are usually **murdered**. If not killed they are harassed, striped of possessions, monitored by CIA and FBI. Some have been so brainwashed by faith groups and biblical passage that they connect any person in this medium as the anti-Christ or their faith requires them to not participate at all. Fear of politics is a learned condition that can be broken and will be broken!

The main purpose of this book is to give an account of my experience when I decided that the above no longer applied to me. The concept of politics being a concrete matter, fixed and unchanging, no longer lived in my mind. The thought of politicians giving the appearance of being untouchable and all-knowing was no longer acceptable to me. The lack of family nobility, royalty, and political inheritance does not exclude us from public service. The idea that money is speech and the working class has no place mentioning policy was eliminated from my brain. The nerve of the idea that an Ivy-League outsider could compete with the collegiate superiors became sickening and disrespectful.

The thought that my seven sons would have to deal with the same concepts because of our family makeup, our background, financial status, and location was unacceptable. As a father, I teach my sons that nothing on this earth is impossible for them. I tell my children about our history. I tell them about American history and American greatness. I also tell them about American mistakes and shortfalls we've had in history. I speak to my children about their abilities and future possibilities.

It didn't occur to me the optimism of the future I painted for them was not their reality. That reality does not exist today and the opportunity for greatness is greatly limited. Like a once tall candle burned to the smallest portion of its wick, that opportunity has faded. We are taught to prepare our children for a world that went extinct 40 years ago. Like a bolt of lightning striking a lonely oak tree, it suddenly occurred to me that our current predicament was solely based on politics and the lack of political will our public servants

4

have had over the years? This has created the narrative for our family's inability to fulfill the dream. The inability to do what is best for the people, country, state, and our future has created a totally ineffective form of government. This type of government is more concerned about elections, political points, and controlling segments of our lives. As this has become a trend so has the decline of the middle class with the decrease in over the last 30 years. College tuition continues to raise over 300 times the amounts 30 years ago. Unemployment begins to level after reaching Great Depression numbers while work force participation is at an all-time low. Globalization continues to take jobs while sleazy American companies leave our shores to headquarter themselves over seas to avoid paying taxes and fair wages. Other dirt bag businesses hide behind religion and waste billions of taxpayer's money in court to a void paying for some birth control for their $8/hr employee.

My God, wake up! The opportunity for competition has been totally taken away. Enough is enough. For the love of country, Alabama, family, and my heritage, I made a conscious decision to offer myself to public service. Being fully aware of the odds and sacrifice I would have to endure in my personal life, I was convinced it was the right thing to do. Sometime we are needed to stand in the gap and show our faith in what's right. Yes there were smarter people, richer people with better name recognition, and better public speakers, but none of them had the courage at the time. I rose to the occasion because I was unafraid of the harsh road ahead. Because my love for my people trumps any fear, giving a voice to the voiceless gave me the all of the bravery needed.

Because I didn't have the name, funding, mentoring, or resources, the "how to" was a mystery. Throughout this book I will take you on my journey to election day. I will discuss in detail my account from not having the financial means and how to be effective throughout a campaign. You will also see chapters related to family with the personal accounts of stress and weathering personal storms of responsibility. Further chapters will discuss constructing a political team and creating the political narrative. Additional chapters will give insight on rolls abilities and effectiveness.

Since campaigns are broken into multiple phases, I will discuss adjustments in a campaign. Also training your mind takes time and action so there are sections dedicated to the subject. You would need to be recognized for your position good or bad. Also included is a chapter on my accounts dealing with Alabama's political parties, politicians, and media. Yes, I'm fully aware that this chapter may not be most reader's favorite, but I will be completely honest in my account. Personal assessments of political machines, marketing groups, get-out-the-vote efforts, and survey effectiveness.

If you read this book I promise you only one thing: you will have my accounts. I will show you evidence that I know unfiltered. From life experience if we learn from each other and perfect ideas, we can become the great nation we all desire and dream to be. Take my fortune or misfortune, build from it. I see life as I see religion or as I see political philosophy, not as a concrete block nor as finished statue, I see it as a living, breathing organism. This idea is of life as incessant lump of clay being steadily molded, but not yet placed into the furnace which creates the final phase into eternity.

In the history of nations there have been many that have deeply affected all subjects of life to push the needle of the human existence further. We learned from our past to better shape our future. from this Blueprint take what you can. If I have error in any way it is OK. Use it to perfect your ambitions. With your days given on this rock live! Do not become complacent; no work is completed on these subjects; they will continue to evolve. Just remember evolution is only possible with the living.

Fool Yourself

Our mind is the greatest tool that we possess; a muscle that uses a fraction of its capabilities to operate the entire body. Our minds can skip in time to see glory ahead and connect with the stars. It has the ability to correct itself, control our body, affect our health, and our personal ability. Our mind is similar to the universe: what we put into it consciously or subconsciously comes back to us in some form. Boomerang!

Like magnetic poles sits good vs. evil, life vs. death, light vs. darkness, black and white, ying and yang, positive and negative. The more positive, good, black or light we put out into the universe the more we received back. The same is true for the opposite; what we receive is the result of what we put out.

With this understanding of our brain, its capabilities and workings, we are able to manipulate ourselves into greatness; hence the phrase, "if you think you can, then you will". Simultaneously, if you think you cannot you eliminate the possibility in your brain that you ever will. This returns to you the failure of the inability you placed into the universe. If you think you are nothing you will only exist as nothing. Just as it works in this form if we train our mind to replace negative thoughts with positive ones, we will have a more successful result. This small talent does not happen overnight like any muscle, the mind yearns for. Give your mind the mental workout it craves! By first learning that our thoughts are real tangible things we can hold on to it. We can see it manifest if we can begin taming the brain.

Secondly, we have to understand the capabilities of the subconscious mind. A simple thought mentioned once a day can develop into desire that turns into a faith to see it exist. Finally, we can have an understanding of the subconscious, we can exercise it by autosuggestion. This is a simple concept of mentioning our thoughts, goals, and desires develop until it becomes reality. Be a detached witness of yourself. Use words of power to control the mind.

To prevent the mind from wandering we must stay focused. When a well is made deep enough it yields water. If you do not use it enough it is only a puddle that will be filled by rain; and in your case, outside distraction. Dreaming or worrying of personal problems only manifests in the subconscious as negative thoughts and results. You are the creator of the day. Visualize it. Know your greatness and go and conquer the day. Voters gravitate to confidence and if you don't act like you are, then they would never believe that you could. Fool yourself.

#JustThinkWright

It was the night of the 2012 presidential election. President Barack Obama had just earned his reelection. There were many first-time candidates on the Republican ticket that also won a substantial number of seats in House of Representatives. One might ask how could the nation vote to reelect a Democrat president, but lose more seats in the House of Representatives. Many Republicans would say that people choose a split government, but a closer glance we see many districts around our nation were designed to keep the minority voice silent.

Before I go any further, I would like to express my revulsion for any political party to rig a district, therefore killing the minority's ability to seek better representation. These devious tactics only increase the discontent of voters and the way they perceive the government. These examples give us a big-definition picture of the true problems as voters. The Nixonian politicians from both the right and left oftentimes work together to sabotage our economic recovery. They fight together to keep the status quo the order of the day. You may say, "my politician would never do that". Please take the crust from your eyes and look for yourself. Wall Street is still making record profits, CEOs bonuses have increased substantially, and the same banks that helped cause the financial meltdown are now 30% larger. They are advocating new legislation preventing safeguards implemented by the Dodd/Frank Act that prevents bad activity and risky investments. More money to the top while we can't make progress on increasing minimum wage. It's the tale of two countries. One is overwhelmingly wealthy while the masses are bearing the heavy burden of lifting; spending less time with their children, workers with no union representation, a household income that is continuously shrinking and let's not forget or fail to mention the tripling cost of education. Massive burdens imposed that makes a young man/woman an indentured servant for the foreseeable future, possibly the rest of their life.

Instead of us voting to change these obvious setbacks, we retreat to our polarized corners and we allow slimy politicians to separate us on issues that have nothing to do with our current conditions. We argue about religion, abortion, same sex marriage, cannabis, and many more. In reality these politicians most likely care nothing about those issue's morality, but understand how to tap dance on your emotions. They laugh in triumph when we make the decisions on hatred the lowest form of who we are.

Here in Alabama, you have people that, in spite of what they do in life, will never see better or be greater. Here in America we have people that can tug on their bootstraps until their hands rain puddles of blood below their feet and would never know a better life. In America you have majority non-white minority populations with no representation. Here we make it more difficult to vote in every election cycle, we continue to gerrymander districts. Both Democrats and Republicans benefit off the voiceless.

8

In the hood (using my urban vernacular) its called being swamped out. It is where you find out it is us against them. The current hierarchy allows life long political seats until his/her body no longer breathes.. One example of being swamped out is right here in Alabama. It happens so often many citizens' and voters see it as the norm. There is one democrat in the House of Representatives from Alabama and the district in which they reside has the largest number of African Americans than any other district in the state. In that district, a democrat is a 100% guaranteed to win that seat. In 2012, the most unbelievable thing happened in the south. The middle of Alabama, the proverbial black belt from the Mississippi line to the Georgia line went completely blue; meaning the demographics in Alabama had shifted. A majority white vote was no longer enough to win elections. One would question if this were the case why did we have such a terrible showing in 2014. Simple redistricting! They swamped us out!

The 2nd Congressional District was one that proved this notion correct. The city of Montgomery which sits in the 2nd Congressional District, includes Montgomery and Lowndes County, had all been in that same district for years. The district had a very large Indigenous African American voting block. In 2014, Montgomery County residents found out the city and counties had been carved like a Thanksgiving turkey, cut into three different congressional seats. Conveniently placing thousands of indigenous voters in the overly heavy African American District 5. This ensured other Republican representatives were a shoe-in for reelection, solidifying their lifetime reign. A hierarchy with no one to answer to. No matter how your politician votes, how bad a job they're doing, or how unconcerned they are about your area, there is no accountability. Equipped with money and new districts that prevent your vote and voice from being heard despite your vote.

As a citizen, as a person that believes in my state, my country and the beautiful people that live here, it is unacceptable to deal with our current state of politics. We the people deserve better and so do our children. If we don't attack this problem our families will suffer!

Let's think "Wright" for a moment! On September 11, 2001 fourth graders at the time, hardly able to understand the tragedy that happened to the towers, have now spent multiple tours in Iraq and Afghanistan or have fallen for our freedom. Ten years later another conflict is brewing in those same areas, but this time my children are the elementary students waiting to be deployed.

In the last 239 years, our country has been at war 222 years with roughly 21years of peace. Colleges have increased tuition every year. Yearly salaries of Americans have decreased. How can I pitch the American dream to my children when that will never be reality, only just a dream? As a parent, how can I do nothing when so many have questions, fears, and concerns? What would that speak about my moral compass if I told my children they can be anything they want if their father is afraid and unwilling to take the duty as the ultimate example? Can you or I wait another 2-8 years before we act to change direction? We will probably wait until we're no longer able to breathe the warm Alabama air without wearing masks. We will probably wait until our fields and farms are barren.; or when we are stamped with a number, a ball and chain with a nice shiny anklet to compliment before we move with urgency. We have to fight against this army of Nixion politicians that turn their noses up at us and see nothing more than sheep because we don't possess the cash and influence to be competitive in this rigged game!

The centering of my moral compass had begun. Then I did more research on the 2nd Congressional District of Alabama. I found I was not the first African American indigenous person that has thought of seeking this office. There was actually a few. There was a person that won this seat; he was one of 3 of the first black Alabama congressman in history. He gained his seat in 1873 during reconstruction. The man, James T. Rapier, was a native of Alabama, born free (like there's any other way to be born?) in Florence, Alabama. Rapier was educated in Tennessee, Canada, and Scotland and afterwards he returned to Alabama. He became a major figure in the Republican Party. James Rapier fought in the black suffrage movement. He became a cotton planter and a true advocate for voting rights. On his return to Alabama he ran for the Alabama Secretary of State in 1870, a race he lost. He won the Congressional Election in 1872, then 1 of 3 indigenous African American congressmen elected from Alabama during Reconstruction. While in Congress, he fought for reparations to African Americans so that they could not only catch up in education, but also have the opportunity to become farmers to cultivate and grow their own towns and businesses. His most famous speech was given in 1874 when he testified for the Civil Rights, which was signed in 1875. Rapier held the treasurer position for the Republican Party and was very vocal about civil rights and economic opportunity for African Americans for eight more years until his death in 1883 in Montgomery, Alabama. He was only 46 years old.

Armed with a sense of urgency, dedication, and slight pride of history I decided with the help of my close circle of loved ones I wanted to do my part in seeking office. Strongly convinced in my mind of duty as a statesman, as an American, as an Indigenous African American, to submit myself for public service. My family, my significant other, and friends didn't expect the type of race I had in mind. Most thought it was a fool's idea because it was nothing local or regional but the United States Congress. Such a tall task with an impossible outcome, the comments would discourage any man. I heard I wasn't smart enough, "you're too poor", "you come from a working class broken family, no party would accept you", "you don't have the time". My friends told jokes about my past. I was reminded my father had cancer and that he had a very troubled past. I was reminded that my mother was only a high school graduate and a museum tour guide. I was reminded that I have 7 sons and they mentioned my child support obligation to one son. They said, "you're a terrible speaker". They mentioned my brother's sexuality and my constant learning of religion and history.

For a moment I questioned myself. What will we get out of this? Will anyone be able to wrap their mind around this? How will I connect? How will I answer personal questions? Will anyone standing with me? Would the incumbent debate their positions? Do we have any other choice? So many questions and no one to answer them. Despite it all my heart was as pure as the moonlit sky. My grandfather a former share cropper and southern Baptist minister, told me once, "whenever you become, lost go to a quiet room and God will help you think right".

I grew up in a very small town. I had never seen a politician, let alone knew how to be one. Because of the aging indigenous population, political leaders have done a horrendous job mentoring and assisting candidates and promoting voter participation. Minority candidates are left to charter the political shark-infested waters alone.

Once the decision to run was concrete, I decided to test the waters to see the public opinion on government and their current congresswoman. Because I didn't have the political backing of older politicians or party, I chose to test the waters in a new way. First I would go to the people. In order to correctly measure the people's discontent with the status quo of government introduced a radical idea and collected signatures for ballot access. I asked the people if I weren't a part of any party would you support me as your next Congressman.

In Alabama, for an independent candidate to obtain ballot access they would have to obtain 12,000 signatures or 10,000 (or 10%) of the popular vote of the last election. This foremost is put in place to prevent anyone outside of the two-party system from participating, basically ensuring the leaders of both parties control who runs for office. No matter how you vote, they were hand-picked already. I am totally against this practice because it builds our distrust for government and officials. On the brighter side, this is what allowed me to enter into the back door to ballot access.

My sons and I loaded the car with snacks and petitions every Saturday. This was the most fun I experienced campaigning we drove city to city speaking with strangers, driving along country roads. Cotton and corn was as far as the eye can see. There were hundreds of forgotten buildings, closed movie theaters, restaurants, hotels and beautiful antebellum homes crumbling because of neglect. Towns once spoken of by presidents as being the best towns in America, now resembled third world countries. Factory after factory boarded up; even the parking lots were beginning to go back to nature with flowers sprouting from the asphalt. The sight of something you truly care for in a dying state is enough to bring any person to tears. The people we met and spoke to often saw "making it" as getting the hell away from Alabama and this hurt my heart deeply.

We once stopped in Florala and met one of the sweetest little ladies I have ever had the pleasure of knowing. She was a local owner of a print shop and miniature golf business and was a local homeowner. I entered her business to print a few flyers to pass around town while we were there. Shocked by my request as a black man in a three-piece suit, she told me that they never done such a thing before. I assured her that she could and we would pay whatever the cost of the ink or paper would be. As the flyers printed, we starting small talking. She was a white, very conservative republican that had lost all respect for government. She even continued to tell me about the glory days of the city. Being a lover of history I indulged in the conversation. The little lady was quite taken by my children's polite manner and my attire. We invited her to lunch and she told us she and her husband own multiple businesses, but during the recession, a lot of businesses flat lined. To make matters worse, her husband was diagnosed with cancer. With no income, she as one of the most prominent people in the town, took a part time job at

Hardees flipping burgers to pay for medicine and treatment for her ill husband. They soon lost their homes and one of their businesses.

I listened and watched her eyes begin to fill with tears as she said, "son, I don't care what color you are or what party you were with. When you make it just think right for us". I gave her my word as a gentleman that I would and I wouldn't forget. As a reminder of this woman's story, I used those words as my first campaign slogan, "just think right". I could feel my grandfather smile in that moment.

After a long day we got back in the car heading to the next location with snacks, beautiful scenery, and our favorite tunes by Frank Sinatra, Tupac, Curtis Mayfield, and John Coltrane.
"Such music seems like a great soundtrack for our mission", my sons would say. My sons didn't quite understand, but they knew their dad was planning to help a lot of people. In their eyes I was a 007-type figure that people told secrets to.

While driving away I cannot put the emotions into words, but I experienced my first taste of political atmosphere and it rivaled the times I ran to cheers while playing football in Demopolis and tearing down the goal post at Troy University; silencing 70,000 people in Death Valley. I found the intersection between finding my life's gift and sharing that gift. I was also quite surprised at how many people were excited about signing the petition. The first week I had over 500 signatures. We went to the football games, family reunions, and church functions. I stood outside nightclubs, black bars and white bars, and every Christmas parade.

Once we participated in a Christmas parade in Enterprise and it was announced in the square who I was and that I wanted their support for Congress. As my sons and I drove by the crowd we waved and said "Merry Christmas" while tossing candy. I looked upon the crowd and what I saw worst that can never be forgotten. I saw cheers of happiness and joy thumbs ups. I saw African American people were shocked, but happy, to see me drive by and for some I saw a terrible grimace on their face. I also saw some that didn't know how to take the news and some looked at me in terrible displeasure like, "I can't believe the audacity of this n*****". Either way, I wanted to be their congressmen and wanted to represent them just like I will represent anyone else, no matter their prejudice. I knew I would get a lot of that on this journey but I'm a grandson of the civil rights movement and a great grandson of ancient Kush.

Another time I was outside of Ozark and I stopped at a small biker's bar to pass out flyers and to get signatures for my petition. as I closed my car door I was told I really didn't want to go into that bar; it wasn't my type of people. I looked up at the person and introduced myself with a grin then and a laugh. I entered into the bar. When I left I received 30 new signatures. I guess it was my type of bar.

Growing up in Alabama you can appreciate good honest racism. At least you know where they stand. I can accept that. You have the right to hate or love whomever you choose. What we can't accept is institutionalize racism that keeps our society crippled and stagnant. In two months we had gathered 5,000 signatures, but with a major deadline looming, I knew I needed help.

I went to Alabama State University and met a young man that was very politically savvy. Steven was the head of the campus democrats, an activist, and a true mover and shaker. I told him about my plan to run for congress, platforms, positions, and the campaign strategy to use coalitions of disgruntle communities to amplify the issues. We also went in-depth about future of Alabama, my goals in my business, and how far we have come up to that point. He laughed and said it was impossible and he would give me the weekend to think it over. I told him I shall think it over, but my decision is final.

Sunday evening Steven gave me a call to schedule the meeting. Monday morning he was my new campaign manager. I received this reaction many times during the campaign. We continued relentlessly to obtain more signatures for ballot access. This did two things: it raised awareness that we were serious about a run for Congress and secondly, because the incumbent was very highly favored, there was a very large chance that other politicians, democrat or republican, would hesitate to step up to the plate. They knew a person was collecting signatures for ballot access and that made a three-way race more challenging than just a head-to-head race with the millionaire incumbent. As the time got closer, the Republicans and Democrats had to declare and register for access. We noticed that no one was willing to run for this office. With 10,000 signatures collected, we decided to run as Democrat. We would pay the required fee and instantly a political nobody was now the Democratic nominee for Congress. This tactic gained us an advantage because we not only deterred any other competition we gain the Democratic base without securing the leadership of the state or country.

We were not hand puppets. We were not bought, paid, nor sold to be in the position. We asked question and the people responded. Without a primary we had the luxury of going straight to the people and campaign on the issues from that day until election night. One may think if you run under a party you automatically have that party's support and resources. This preconceived notion is far from reality. I learned over the course of the campaign if you were not completely wealthy or if you didn't have a political name or lineage; the National Democratic Party and state party will be absolutely no help. One could also say that if the party leaders do not have a connection to the people. nothing they could do what hip. This goes back to the concept that I do not believe anyone should expire while in office. In Alabama we have the problem that party leadership has been in place for so long that they no longer understand or know the wants, desires, or principles of the people they are attempting to represent.

Previous tactics and tricks that worked in the 70s, 80s, and 90s do not work with today's voter. I found the Democratic leadership to be useless. I also found that the National Party was also useless, not because they were unable to fundraise and receive donations, but they were useless because of the unpopular decisions and current political environment that the president received in the south.
Democrats have a knack for preaching programs and issues, but they are terrible at telling the public their positions based on conviction and moral standing politics should be more

values than programs. Because of this there is a disconnect southern Democrats have with the voters that they want to represent. Below the Mason Dixon line, every border is slightly conservative in some fashion because of their personal beliefs, morals, and value systems. Because of this, national political figures, including the President, were largely absent in the south and did not campaign or assist many newcomers to politics. They played the safe bet with bank-owned voters turning out based on rhetoric and pet projects. You could say that the party was destroyed desperately by searching for a voice but found none.

On the state level, my encounters with the party under which I ran was, what I can only describe as disconnected. I did not ruffle any feathers or take on anyone in my party. I accepted help if they had any to give, and I was willing to help in any way I could to spread the message based on values to the southern voters. No matter how eagerly I was willing to help, the party itself did not have the funds, resources, or material to assist new candidates over the course of the campaign. I had a chance to meet many bright, young, up-and-coming political stars. Some were so qualified for the positions they were running for, that it was inconceivable how anyone could vote against them. If only they took a second to listen to the things these candidates had to say or even viewed their qualifications.

I met a former soldier that served multiple tours abroad fighting for our freedom against terrorism. His firsthand knowledge on military procedure, assessment of risk, and how our country is viewed beyond our borders made that young Democrat a candidate either party could back. With a grassroots effort and a keen sense of constituents concerns, he also ran into the problem of a disconnected party, lack of resources, manpower, and plain old lack of support. Other candidates I met would be a shoe-in, but because their message went unheard by so many, it was hard for them to get the support needed even though they were the right person for the job. I can only blame this on leadership. You cannot do the same thing for 40 years and not expect to adapt to the changing times. The party leadership is the brain of the state body of constituents. Unfortunately, in Alabama the brain is on life support and can hardly sustain life I am not sure if it is because of arrogance or laziness that the party does not welcome new leadership or young voices. The party acts with no regard to changing times and changing political narratives. Many great ideas often fall on deaf ears. It would be understandable if the plan of leadership was a plan for success and we can see it being tangibly put forth. It has not in Alabama and the Republican Party has a supermajority in the wings of politics and the governors position. Its virtually impossible for democrats to gain traction. Instead of finding new and innovative ways to bring people under the tent, they only find ways to shun people to make them switch party and protect their own interests.

Take the annual celebration to commemorate Martin Luther King Jr. Selma to Montgomery March, for example. You have individuals, politicians, activists, actors, community leaders, the rich, and well known gathered all in one Alabama city. They take the podium they wave their hands, point their finger and speak until they are hoarse. They sweat profusely and scream how we will stop people from trampling on our ability to vote. They speak on how they will stop violence and poverty. They speak on everything they can do for the community while they do their best Southern Baptist pastor imitation while just across the street there are housing projects with oblivious to the mayhem the political elite.

I watched as a large political figure gave a speech so powerful, but knew the absence of physical solutions. Right across the street you have children with no shoes on, you had fights break out, you have people with no money in their pockets and no possibility for a job to have a better life. You see buildings crumbling and streets filled with debris and trash. Then I glanced at your favorite politicians with $10,000 suits, joined hand and arm, singing "we shall overcome" while walking the sacred pilgrimage just for the cameras and sound bites. This goes to show that the African American wing of politics it's quite petty in their concept of profiting off the Civil Rights Movement. Amusingly, we have been warned about this type of leech before.

Booker T. Washington once said, "there is another class of colored people who make a business of keeping the troubles, the wrongs, and the hardship of the negro (indigenous) race before the public. Having learned that they are able to make a living out of their troubles, they have grown into the settled habit of advertising their wrongs—partly because they want sympathy and partly because it pays. Some of these people do not want the negro (indigenous) to lose his grievances, because they don't want to lose their jobs". I often wondered if their catalog of words to use in public were only those that could make people feel convicted enough to vote or shame them enough to tell them that they should vote because somebody gave their lives for you to have the opportunity. I do not hear politicians of other races push this argument to their constituents as the sole reason why one should. People vote when they're educated enough to vote and when people understand the magnitude of a vote. When we understand the issues we can grasp a better understanding of what politics can do to our lives.

Politics effects everything from our jobs, to our state our city in the air we breathe and the food that we eat. People will vote if they have the information. So the biggest thing we can do is search for those people and give them the information and in return they to vote. To leadership this may be an outlandish statement: you can't stay silent and invisible, then send letters to tell people how to vote. This may have worked 30 years ago when more of the population were illiterate and most of the population did not have information at their fingertips.. In today's society, to be successful politically in the South, one must have face-to-face interaction and there is no substitute for that. I understand that this may come as a cost, but if we collect money only to give to the leech for them to do nothing, why give money in the first place? Also if there was year round education on the issues you wouldn't have that much convincing to do during election time.

Qualifying day is what's upon us as we sit back and wait to see if there would be any other candidates willing to jump in the race. The brilliance of announcing early and announcing and as a independent candidate deterred any democrats because they did not see it possible to beat the incumbent.. This plan hailed true at 12:00 p.m. on qualifying day. There wasn't a single politician willing to challenge the two-time incumbent. Out of all of the rhetoric, arguments, discontent not a single democrat, republican, independent, or libertarian wanted to qualify. And this was also the same for other congressional districts and statewide races.

Time: 2:00 p.m. on qualifying day and not a soldier willing. I saw a young who was said to be an up and coming figure in the state politics. He was a tall Euro-American man, maybe in his mid-30's, blue suit and wore glasses. If I were to guess his profession, I would say attorney or an accountant. He entered into the democratic headquarters and asked if anyone had qualified for a particular race. He found out no one was willing to challenge one of the most hated and controversial politicians in the state. He stood tall and unbuttoned his suit jacket. With his index finger he pushed his glasses closer to his eyes, his left hand was placed on his waist, and told the party rep, "if no one qualifies by 3:00 p.m., I'll run against him, myself". I admired the young man's tenacity. I was told that his family has been very dedicated to Alabama politics, and just as he said, at 3:00 p.m. he returned to qualify. I introduced myself to him and told him good luck. He smiled and said, "same to you and I like that tie". I laughed as he left the building. I was still in a bit of a shock at the amount of people that they were going to have no opposition. I thought to myself, "are we, the public, that unconcerned that we are willing to give anyone a position without any accountability?" Damn, free money! I could not run for every position but I could find people that would! I reached out to young men and women across the state; I found a handful of concern citizens would take up an almost impossible challenge.

By 3:30p.m. we had the largest number of Indigenous African Americans in the state of Alabama to run for office since reconstruction. These individuals were not by any means placeholders or the known heir-apparent. It amuses me to think of those lost souls that based their campaign on Obama and hatred. Most incumbents had nothing to say and they most certainly would not stand before the citizens and explain their actions. Power with no accountability. Take former Alabama Governor Robert Bentley, for example, advertised himself as a job creator and cutter of taxes, upon reelection, his first order of business was to raise the taxes on Alabama citizens. His opponent in the 2014 election carried a large 15-foot inflatable duck to every city in Alabama, challenging the governor in a debate. I could attribute to the fact that incumbents spent more money "ducking" opponents; they would never attend a debate or forum. Even if the debate is held by the largest schools, universities, or military bases in the state, they did not attend. We often debated ourselves on issues and took on a bombardment of questions and concerns from the public that were currently falling on deaf ears. Political races in 2014 seemed so uneven on the face, but given more attention you could see the political newcomers were smart, bright, and gutsy. They were also resourceful, because they all lacked was the huge donor support. Instead of advertising in newspaper or hard copy, everything was done via Internet by dominating social media and small local settings. Alabama's state auditor race should baffle any practically thinking person. The citizens had the option to vote for a candidate with years of auditing experience untainted by politics, young, energetic, and a woman or a candidate with no experience or education background for the job that has lost 10 political races. Guess who got elected? That's right, the more green of the two for reasons that can only be described as stupidity and party politics.

I met an army veteran that had the idea that the only way to look out for his fellow comrades and get them the care and attention they needed was to take the charge against his current congressman. My God, I never saw a congressman work so hard to discredit a man with hardly any political clout! I could tell they were worried shitless.

I received my first attack of my political career just a few days after qualifying. I woke up that morning to calls from the NY Daily News, UK Daily News, Huffington Post and they even had a segment about me on FOX News. In just three days I went from being a political nobody to the only Alabama politician to receive national and international coverage. The local news affiliates were somewhat hot and called on the conservative news outlet The Yellow Hammer News. The article they published gave them national recognition, even though they painted me to be a mindless guy with no political future. One should question if this is so, why give me the publicity? Furthermore how was it possible for them to save a YouTube video that I deleted well over a year before qualifying? Easy, they all knew I existed. This just goes to show when you think people are not watching you or your message is not getting through it is, trust me. In the video I sat on a toilet and gave my thoughts on infringement of rights. Yes, I mentioned abortion. In the Bible Belt that could be political suicide, but I stuck to my guns. In America we have laws and a constitution, if you don't like or agree with either get the political will up enough to change it and don't try to crucify me for stating the facts. Besides, I have seven lovely boys. Obviously for my family, abortion was not an option. Ninety seven percent of my statement were affirmed by Fox and other political pundits. Living in today's society, where social media can touch the world only if you give them the shocking, outrageous, and drama filed bait then you can capture the attention of the world. My scenery and title to the video may have been left field, but the ideas were not. Even if I looked like a buffoon, I knew political attention spans and memories are very short. Hell, in Alabama we have politicians under investigation and they still win in landslide victories. I left bread crumbs and they ate them hook, line, and sinker. I was confident that once anyone saw my information and what I stood for it would not matter.

Once I secured the democratic nomination, we got to know some the democratic leaders. We were able make connections in 14 counties and I planned on visiting all them. Sticking to the plan we met all democrats at the Alabama democratic conference and the new south coalition affiliates. These meetings are total mixed bag location could be a 3 star hotel in Birmingham to and a1870 schoolhouse. The first time I met the chairman of the Democratic Party was in Ozark at a banquet. I introduced myself to her and expressed my eagerness to work with the party in order to drive voter participation. She explained she would do what she could. Never heard from her, or Democratic Party.

The great people of Greenville allowed me a moment to speak when the chairman was in attendance and I remember the line she spoke, "democrats believe in jobs, affordable health care, and education". These are my words about that speech: yes, we believe in jobs healthcare and education, but we also believe in standing up for ourselves and fighting for the future we would like to see. If we lay down if we do the bare minimum we will remain in last place.

The final contact I had with Madame Chairman was by way of voicemail the day after the election to let me know I did a great job and ran a respectable race and to remember that sometimes the best people do not always win.

In the first conversation with the head of the Alabama Democratic Committee said, "son you better have some money, or know where to find it. Good luck!" I laughed to myself and told him thank you for the advice.

The largest university in the second congressional district is Troy University and my opponent has spoken at the graduation commencement. She has multiple photos, connections, and has expressed very heart felt agreeance with the chancellor, faculty and staff. This institution is also my alma mater (Go Troy!). The University invited both candidates to an open floor debate. It was spearheaded by faculty and students. For a moment I was nervous, but after coming to my better judgment, I thought of a quote from the Art of War. Suh Zu said, "know thy self and know thy enemy dare not fear losing thousands battles." We have studied my opponent, we have learned the weaknesses, we have regurgitate the facts so many times I say them off shear autosuggestion. The enemy was known, and if the battle were to be fought victory was certain. Foolish of me to think she would appear. I spent the entire night throwing high fives to an Alabama House of Representatives candidate. Even he had an amazing shot of winning, his opponent also did not show. We took a barrage of questions from the professors and students on the issues that they were most concerned about. Even though the voting participation of this group is relatively low, it is the same block of people that will be in the workforce and affected by decisions we make today. They asked questions from gun rights, gay rights, marijuana, mass incarceration, death penalty, the ability to upgrade the grid, and countless other concerns. They were met with full discussion and engagement! I didn't look down on them, look away, or criticize about the topics. I expressed the current position, what was possible, what could be done and what is a fallacy. The attendees thanked me for my honesty and my straightforwardness. We opened up a box of greatness with the people that had the audacity to think about the things that are possible. They bought into an idea that we aren't alone in our thinking and feelings. We have the consensus if we only speak out, we will see we are the majority. Lucky for Martha Roby she did not attend the night would have ruin her game of charades.

We had a regimen we stuck to religiously because our budget wasn't large enough for the typical marketing of television, prime time radio, saturated markets of blog sites, and newspapers. We were small and untraceable and that was our niche, to reach the votes of the 2nd Congressional District. We were a breath of fresh air and the opposite of Washington D.C. With this advantage, the convenience of multiple vehicles, and the ability to be on the road fulltime, I could be in Dothan at 9 a.m., and by 7p.m. we made our way to Millbrook. We had developed 6 routes that would take us to multiple cities and back to Montgomery with a 6 a.m. departure and a 2 a.m. return. We did the opposite of many politicians today; we campaigned like George Wallace or Big Jim Folsom. We wanted to meet any and everyone.

One of my guilty pleasures during my campaign was my admiration and appreciation of the scenery. Satisfying my inner nerd, I took in the sites of absolutely gorgeous homes along my trail; the Antebellum historic homes that should be preserved and renovated for educational use. I saw them in the saddest condition; some practically dilapidated. I enjoyed Andalusia's downtown and the catfish restaurants; downtown Greenville with the theater lights blaring in the night, giving you remnants of the 1920s; Georgiana's downtown with train tracks and stores, and the diversity of the wiregrass; Enterprise with its wonderful mix of people from a host of racial identities living and steadily growing; Dothan with its great murals, art, culture, and such progressive thinking.

I think back during the campaign we were in Dothan where we met an artist that was creating a new mural of his reflection of diversity of the city. The ending result was breathtaking; a rosy-cheeked girl with golden blonde hair, an older gentleman with shiny grey whiskers, a mother and daughter, and a guy smiling from ear to ear with glasses (me). At the same location, a wedding party arrived to take a few photos. I approached the couple to congratulate them on their union. The couple was a business owner and an IT specialist. They informed me that they wanted to take pictures here to remember their home, because they are moving to Arizona. They expressed the inability to find a job in the IT field in Alabama and one expressed the red tape and taxes imposed on entrepreneurs. All seemed like valid reason for leaving the state, but the main reason why they were leaving was the married couple were both women.

The entire cities of Union Springs and Eufaula showered us with so much love we began to think of them as home. We were adopted time and time again by so many families that it is impossible to name them all.
We avoided most of the mainstream outlets and focused more on the tools to bring us closer to voter's hearts. Surveys and polls were useless we were creating our own support. By being apart of the people, we found ourselves on the frontline of major topics in the state, and brought more publicity to the fight.

At 1 a.m., after a long day of campaigning and traveling, we got word of a group of workers on strike for fair treatment. We were told they were going to be picketing day and night. I thought to myself, "anyone that would fight for their rights to be treated fairly was definitely people I had to meet and support". These workers weren't asking for more money, they were asking to be treated like men and women.

Exhausted already, I told my trusted friend and advisor, Nelson Jancanarino, "take us to the closest fast food place". I ordered 50 chicken sandwiches and we drove to meet those workers. We were greeted with open arms. We sat and listened, laughed, joked, some cried, and others were so shocked that a would-be politician was out so late with no cameras around. They told me to go get some sleep and I took their advice since it was 4 a.m. and home was three hours away. Needless to say, by 11 a.m. the following day I returned to answer questions about insurance changes in their contracts. One worker told me I was a machine, I told him we are on a mission I don't get tired! In a right to work state, where most people are employed at will, the union we stayed up with never supported us in the end. Talk about politics as usual!

As much as we traveled, met voters, and gained people's trust, we were faced with so many difficulties. During the campaign trail I was giving a speech in Millbrook and my cellphone began to ring over and over again. After I finished speaking, I stepped away to receive the news my uncle, Wilbur Wright, had passed away. This would be an unfortunate reoccurring theme throughout the campaign. Just a few months later, I was being pinned by an Army official as they gave me a minute to say my final farewells to one of my best friends and brother, Sgt. Rogger Webb. Three tours in Iraq and two tours in Afghanistan could not break my brother, but a malfunction of his motorcycle in Kanas took my brother away. That same day I gave a very emotional speech to in Dothan. No time to grieve. I could only play back the last voicemail he left saying, "my Negus! You gonna shock the world, man! All that reading finally paying off! (Laughs) Give them hell and don't back down. They send us to war, but they ain't never bust a gun. I'm with ya brother. One! Chaaaa!" No tears to shed, I campaigned harder!

Unfortunately, the old saying about bad things happening in threes came true during the month of August. Traveling to make a speech in front of the largest crowd I had ever addressed, I was informed that my father lost his 4 year battle with lung cancer. My father, Richard Wright, was a machine operator for 20 years, a mechanic and janitor at John Carroll University. He lived a very hard life between poorly ventilated factories, drug and alcohol abuse, and poor diet. This man worked extremely hard until the day he died. Three siblings and myself survived him. Such terrible news to receive, the worst of which was my father spent his every possession on his treatments. Father cashed his 401k and all savings attempting to buy more time to be with his children and grandchildren. The business of cancer is the worst with medicines that kill and cost a fortune. This only left the massive burden on his eldest son, me. It was said that the speech I gave was so moving that they compared me to names I dare not insult by mentioning, but every word came from my heart directly to the hearts of everyone in attendance.

November 4, 2014: Election Day was finally here! We had poll watchers and volunteers in 14 counties. Each leader reported to our campaign almost up to the hour. I was fully aware that the race would be decided solely on voter turn out. If people voted in large numbers the chances of a win increased by 90%, but if turnout was low we were guaranteed to lose by default. We did everything we could to reach the people, now we would sit back and wait. (Laughs) We would absolutely not! We came up with a plan in Montgomery to get the attention of nonparticipants and give some lighthearted humor to those that did do their civil duty. Once again shocking the public with the unthinkable, we purchased Captain America costumes and carried #JustThinkWright signs. We rotated from precinct to precinct, bringing smiles and salutes to men women and children. We went to local stores reminding them to vote, we walked in restaurants, we stood by the highway greeting all that passed. The look in people's eyes was of pride, optimism, and joy. By 2 p.m. we had already made it on every news outlet from Montgomery to Norfolk, Virginia. After running for miles, jumping, saluting, waving, hugging, and taking pictures we cast our ballots. As my team and I sat at our watch party, I told everyone how proud I was of them and how happy I was that they believed in what we have accomplished and regardless of outcome we did the impossible being here. The polls were closed numbers began to come in one after another, amusingly they called the

Alabama governor races merely seconds after the polls closed. It was the fastest call in Alabama history. That wasn't a great sign, considering the gubernatorial candidate was on the same ticket we were. Voter turnout was abysmal, the worst in over 40 years. After 45 grueling minutes, the race was called. We listened to the commentator say this would be a totally different outcome if voter turnout was different. They, too, were expecting an upset. "Not this day", I addressed the crowd in attendance telling them, "to not accept what's given, but get out and make a change. You don't need a million dollars to be heard. Get involved because the people that represent us now hold the keys to what our future looks like. We lost the race, but we will never lose that fire for a better tomorrow".

Sure there were countless things I could have done better or differently. If I had more money more time more help and again more money. Like they say in the hood "if if was a 5th ,we would all be drunk." I don't regret a single thing! We gave it all that we had and much more. That same feeling I had the first day only grew 1,000 times over. It allows me to neither quit nor be silent. Alabama deserves better! We deserve better and until this body expires I will not stop, give up, give in, or go easily into the night! #JustThinkWright!

Alabama Political Environment

The easiest thing in the world anyone can do when faced with a problem is place blame and stick to the most familiar arguments. Usually these actions often bear the same miniscule results. The more an difficult action when faced with a problem would be to welcome change. To do something different and accept responsibility for the state of affairs in the institution. The only true wisdom in life is that there will always be change and change must happen for progress. Politics in the state of Alabama is a sector of our life that yearns, begs, for change, but because of certain forces it continues to be as stubborn as mule mascot. The concrete, never-changing politics only wills its own destruction. The two party systems of Democrat and Republican rule the narrative of Alabama politics. This makes a clear divide between people and causes the "us against them" mentality. In the mind of the voters it only makes it impossible for true leadership to be developed from any person outside of the political elite. Voters Run to their polar opposites based on family, history, tradition, and religion.

In this chapter, I will not discuss in any detail the Republican Party of Alabama simply because they have proven (super majority and the governor position) to everyone that supports them that they are the party of the rich. Their word means nothing. They are absolutely corrupt and intellectually challenged on the subject of governing. My firsthand experience is with the Democratic Party of Alabama, so I will stick to my observations that I have seen inside the party and the information I've gathered from citizens across the state of Alabama.

When further dissecting Alabama's Democratic Party, one could sum up in three main reasons for the party's downfall and struggle to find traction with voters.

The first reason is people like to be on a team, but they don't want to be on a team splintered into cliques and cells. The Alabama Democratic Party, the Alabama Democratic Conference, County Democrats, ADC County Democrats, Empower Alabama, New South Coalition, and so on all are splinters of one single party. No team can be successful in fractions. In sports, every position has a certain role to play and when each player handles their responsibilities the team moves forward and is highly successful. This is true in every sense of shared responsibility. The battery starts the engine, the engine moves the car, and the driver steers. All working together will take you collectively to your destination. Sadly, in the Democratic Party in Alabama, everyone wants to be the driver and no one wants to accept the responsibility as the battery, the engine, or the brakes. In short, there are chiefs, but no Indians. There are majors and generals, but no soldiers.

The second reason for the democrat's problems is communication. Lack of communication and vision between party chair, county officials, and the public has desensitize voters and increased what grey collars call "voter apathy". Each faction is set for failure by being a independent player moving at different speeds and not in unison.

The State Democratic Chair should be lively, should participate should be 90% travel, should be active in every county, should be open for communication, and campaigns year-round to convince them about the moral standing and values of the party. Recruiting should start at the high school level and you should want the brightest and most politically aware. Recruiting should be on the same level as athletic recruiting. If a team wanted some solid players and playmakers they would write, call, and visit students regardless of their name or parental influence. Instead we allow media, prisons, and the streets to do more recruiting and they are winning the battle whole-heartedly. The Chair should visit high schools, colleges, and nursing homes to ensure that everyone knows of the party's principles and there should be symposiums and workshops weekly. The next step is mentoring of candidates while on the campaign trail. There should be weekly calls, updates on new information the party has to offer, list of potential volunteers, voter list, and list of party sponsored events, and social media presence. The local county chairs should have the same job description as to state chair, just county-specific.

The third reason for the Democrats difficulties in Alabama politics is disconnection. I need to provide disclosure and ask that you please receive my next statements with love and respect for all mentioned. The disconnection between state chair and public cannot be repaired. The state chair is knowledgeable and would be a great advisor. The Chair has a huge resource of knowledge that should always be available to future candidate and members of the Democratic Party. To be successful, a Chair should be younger, healthier, eager, and more grassroots connected. The same can be noted about county chairs, with the current age ranging from 65 to 85. With the average age of voters ranging from 21 to 45, there are decades between voters and party chairs this is the disconnection that is so evident.

There is also a huge disconnection with a large population of indigenous black voters. the disconnection is between the entities that claim to speak for this section of the voters. It was clear and obvious after the 2014 midterm elections that these groups are only able to reach less than 20% of the indigenous black population, leaving 80% of the population deaf to the group's message. Last minute sample ballots and constant civil rights rhetoric does not reach the voters intended. I'm sure this tactic work perfectly 20 to 30 years ago. Today it is not enough! If these groups are to be successful going forward, there has to be more than talk amongst themselves. There must be education among the population of voters. Engagement must be visible and more than just during election cycles. These groups must develop collegiate chapters and think tanks to recruit future generations. They must be willing to add more people to the voting rolls even if it means that they cannot control the outcome of their vote. If your organization and the leaders are too old to do the legwork needed there are (as you know in this hard fought economic environment) 10 applicants for every one job opening. There are no excuses! More than capable people are ready and willing. The groups also contribute to voter disconnection with continual reference of black and white. I cringe and hold my head when I hear grey collars use the words "voter apathy", "whites of good will", "poor whites", "poor blacks", and "mean-spirited whites". These terms are outdated and very much passé words that should be eliminated from our political vernacular. Although well intentioned, these words no longer have a place in our society. They're clear examples of older generations ignoring changing times. Society has evolved to eliminate such words like "retard" replaced by "intellectual disability", "sissy" or "fag" for "gay or LGBT, "nigger" for "Indigenous" (the term African American removes your rights by DNA and by soil).These words give people the respect and dignity that they deserve. Even the flamboyant hip-hop generation uses less inflammatory words. They have replaced the word "bitch" with less vulgar "thot", and "pussy popping" with "twerking".

It would be safe to say that the indigenous politicians, or the African American politicians, in the last 50 years have been the largest downfall in urban society. The final, but most important disconnection between the political black elite and black voters, is the black church no longer speaks for the black majority and they will not allow civil rights era to end so that the fight for natural rights can begin. Grey collars have incased their politics with the cover of civil rights, proving more interested in remembering cliff note events from one era in our extremely long history on this planet, than the developing one that we live in currently. They tell the black indigenous community to be thankful for civil rights for all that we are today. The majority of indigenous black Alabamians resent this notion. It reeks of the days slave owners and Uncle Tom's preached their version of the Bible, to tell you that to be subservient was the order of the day. It reeks of days we were told our ancestors were primitive animals with no sense of culture or education. This disconnection is very dangerous because as black indigenous citizens become more educated, the gap between political leaders and the masses of black voters grows farther and farther apart. Like the slave and the slave master, people will begin to develop their own versions of politics; just like the slaves did with the twisted form of religion taught by slave owners.

You can see this how disconnected black leadership is by merely looking at the 2016 presidential election. You have the civil rights (politicians and pastors) vanguard that endorsed and actively campaigned for Hillary Clinton months before she declared to run. Meanwhile, the millennials backed Bernie Sanders and have very low expectation of Hillary's capabilities to actually create the change that's yearned for. Indigenous communities around Alabama aren't concerned about a return of segregation, slavery, or KKK. Most feel they never left. Others, well I would dare anyone of any race to tell a young black male to move to the back of the bus or go tell a young black (indigenous) person that they cannot enter into the front doors of any place of accommodation. I laugh to myself, because this will never happen. Society is very much afraid of black (indigenous) men.

For all the tremendous work that was done in the civil rights era, there were short falls. We as a people were so focused on ending segregation that we didn't prepare for integration. We were so focused on being United States citizens that we knowingly or unknowingly gave up our natural rights by DNA and by land. Secondary or artificial citizens of 13th and 14th amendment, not natural born citizens of the United States; the original constitution was clear that could only be white males. Women didn't get a chance to vote till the 50's and indigenous people didn't receive true access till after 65. We could be recognized in similar manner as Native Americans, which most are not truly native at all. What we currently see is a group of Europeans posing as a tribal while their DNA reeks of England, Ireland, and France. We could own casinos, have our own police department, territory land and still be considered citizens. Desegregation meant only one thing: indigenous (black) people no longer had to do for themselves. Yes, what your seeing is correct. In my assessment, desegregation was more harmful than helpful. The truth is in the sharp decline in black gas stations, banks, movie theaters, hospitals, and schools. They have all closed.

When speaking to a group of young men I asked if their future plans in life are to go to college and find a job. We have to be the only people in the world that educate themselves just to become someone's slave. I asked one young man, "would you like to build your own car brand or open a bank," he replied, "no, sir. That will never happen". I told the young man, "when you walk in the bank do black people work in that bank?" "Yes". "Why can't they run their own bank? In Alabama Hyundai employees are over 80% black, so why cant indigenous people build their own cars to sale?" The young men sat silent for moment, then a one raised his hand and said, "I am going to own a train that doesn't need tracks". That's how ignorance is erased. Instead we traded our God-given birth right to become secondary citizens and property of the state in which we live. A state we find to still be recognized in as slaves. There should be no shock when we are treated as property by police. If you take a look at your license your name reads in all caps, which denote property of. Because I am indigenous American of Moorish-Kushite descent, I can speak clearly on the subject. The term "African American" is bullshit. The Olmecs were in the Americas thousands of years before Columbus landed on the island outside of Cuba. Furthermore, Columbus didn't discover America, hell, he never stepped foot in a single state in the union. The truth of the matter is land was taken, history erased, women were raped, babies were killed, people were drowned in the ocean, and homeowners that had trades, families, and businesses were taken from their indigenous homeland. Dumb, ignorant animals cannot navigate ships through the vial of darkness. Naked savages with no intelligence cannot build houses nor teach plantation owners how to grow crops.

It is well documented the accomplishments of indigenous people. I will not apologize nor sidestep the facts about history, and for that reason I won't allow the blatant destruction or distortion of history to benefit a few. When this is allowed we suffer from failing schools, high unemployment, violence, lack of opportunity, pothole roads, and crumbling bridges. Our family structure and accountability for who we are has not been our primary focus. If we allow this to continue we ensure only what we have always received: a population of people that continue to be the oil that runs the machine of their demise. In order to progress one must do something progressive, out of the ordinary, spontaneous, "shock" and "wow". If your city or state resembles the previous mentioned, then we are suffering from a similar circumstance.

Unfortunately, the keepers of the Civil Rights Movement have done just that for over 40 years and we have suffered in every statistical category. Stevie Wonder once wrote a song that said, "if you believe in things you don't understand, you'll suffer. Superstition ain't the way." If we deal in superstition how can we ever face the facts of reality?

Because there are no visible chains we share is a false illusion of freedom, therefore we live in a warped sense of reality. Instead of building for the future, we have lived off the hard work of the past. Instead of fighting for perfection of our rights, we pretend as if we have arrived at the promised land we heard so much about. I'm not calling specific names but the numbers and statistics show the disconnection we have with our demographic. As for solutions, we must stop waiting to put out fires. We must start fires ourselves with bold stances on legalization of cannabis, bold stances on net metering, bold stances on college affordability, anti-violence, fair pay, international trade agreements and business opportunities, text book revisions, and on pro athletics. This is a small list of the few things people will stand with you lock in step. I truly believe the Alabama is interested in all of the above, and if they are willing to take up the fight, there is a soldier in myself ready to lend my sword and shield.

Get in the race

Mentor to a student, knight to a squire, artist to apprentice, and a king to a prince; these examples show great transfer of knowledge from one person willing to teach and the next willing to learn. It is customary that this is done in hopes that the new keeper of knowledge will use it to his advantage and cherish it to their best ability. Perfecting inferiorities of the design and passing on for additional perfection. Making the trade exact to with the next person willing to take up the charge. Unfortunately politics is a field that those who are lucky enough to know the process and the techniques do not freely give the information. They keep such tight lips that one would think you would have to have a members-only jacket be inducted into some sort of secret society or possess some secret decoder ring for information that should be coming and accessible to everyone. That is only a trick, a trick to discourage you from following your heart of public service! Don't worry, I have composed information in this chapter that will get you started on the right political track.

First, we must build your political knowledge. Politics has been around for many years you can find political movements dating as far back as Umayaa to Egypt, Rome, Italy, France, and other places. There are hundreds of political ideologies you don't have to know all of them. It helps to have a foundation of knowledge. Running for political office is often very time consuming. With knowing this fact, a person must be dedicated to the idea with no chance for retreat. The great coach Larry Blankney often mentions burning our boats and storming the castle on the hill. For on that battlefield you can give it your all, no matter the outcome. There was no possibility of evacuation only to stand and conquer. If the opposing coaches, Nick Sabin or Lou Holtz, it didn't matter to the players because we prepared, we trained and we learned. We could step into any arena and be known as equals or better. Therefore, when we enter the game of politics we must prepare. How is this done with no coaches to assist, no one to reference, no access to funds to produce them? In my case, I had absolutely neither so I gathered texts from our past.

All people have suffered genocide. We must read and understand them all. The Holocaust, Christopher Columbus and African/indigenous Holocaust, Haiti, Congo, and indigenous Americans gives us a better understanding of people and how we can operate with understanding going forward. I would be hard pressed to say that we have truly done our homework on past events. When we accomplish this task the better understanding of people take place. So read, listen, and write down your accounts. Your attempt is the building block for someone else to walk in your footsteps and beyond.

I suggest you start with the classics to better understand the joys. The brutalities and the manipulations. You will need to understand the advancements of political thoughts and ideas that have been created in our history. The best reference for this is "The Prince" by Niccolo Machiavelli. His political strategy dealt with the most animalistic natures we can find in our human DNA. He explains how one should be of two people, able to do the good and wouldn't hesitate when time presents itself to do badly. This would cause a positive result, even if the immoral act was to be done. The author explains this theory by saying a man should be of both natures. He used analogies of the fox and the lion. He stated one must be a fox so that you can recognize traps, and also a lion so that you can have the strength to do what is needed to be done.

Now politics has come a very long way from the backstabbing nature of Machiavelli's writings but you can still find remnants in people's nature and politician's actions. The next thing once you learn those, is how to create a political movement in order to run for office. The best reference point that I can give you related to this subject will be found in the book called the *Perfect Politician*. The text is set in 1945 and it explains how certain politicians were able to capitalize on the discontent for current representation and the issues that each segment of the population had. The book called this concept "the coalition of minorities". When creating a political movement, you must know what the issues are driving the people you would like to represent. I should note that no one person can have the same passion about one issue as others. You have gay rights activists, marijuana legalization activists, energy activists, conservation activists, and so on. But, if you can embody a plan that includes all of the following of the previously stated, you turn a group of few into a coalition of many people. I would like to note that there are many books and reference points on these subjects. I've only given you the books I have found the most helpful to me.

The next resource I would encourage you to have, is a book on constructing campaign strategy and how to get yourself in a mental state of strategic planning. The text most often used and was read multiple times by myself, is the *Art of War* by Sun Tzu.
Now that we have gained some foundational information, the next thing you must do is pick a race to run. The easiest thing is to pick the straw man and burn it to the ground. I should tell you to do the most conservative and safe thing by starting in a local city or municipal race then work your way up to run for higher positions, but damn that! I did not take that, advice and if you have the know-how and education you shouldn't either. I only know that only you can be the judge of what race is right for you. Don't allow anyone to tell you differently. I would say remember the larger the race,, the more time, the more money, the more information, and the more travel is needed so please keep this in mind. Take an inventory of the wrongs and rights that you feel the most strongly about in your city, your state, and in your country. This inventory would give you a better idea of what race may interest you the most. There are so many positions that you can run for. The following is a list of positions and job descriptions just waiting for you to take up the charge.

(Not Alabama-specific)

State Senator: The State Senate consists of representatives who are elected in districts that usually span several cities and counties. State Senators are usually more high-profile political campaign candidates and their terms last longer than those of State Representatives or State Assemblymen.

State Representative/State Assemblyperson: The State House of Representatives, or State Assembly as it is called in some states, generally consists of members who are elected from districts for terms of two years. Like the State Senate, they are among the highest-profile local political campaigns. The position of State Assemblywoman/State Representative is usually considered part-time and requires weekly visits to the Statehouse for voting and government business.

Democrat/Republican State Central Committee: A person from each party (Democrat and Republican) are elected in each State Senate district. These State Central Committee members meet at the state capitol a few times a year and make decisions about party matters, such as electing party leadership and Chairperson.

Board of County Commissioners: The position of County Commissioner is usually a full-time position with a term of four years. There are most often three commissioners on a board and usually everyone in the county can vote in the election. Some counties, though, may have more than three commissioners and they may be elected in different districts within a county.

County Executive: Some counties have an elected County Executive in addition to, or instead of, County Commissioners. The County Executive, if elected, is voted upon by the entire county.

County Auditor: This position is appointed in some counties, but is a elected office in most with a four-year term. It is usually held by someone with accounting and auditing experience, but most counties allow anyone to run for the full-time office.

County Engineer: Many states only allow certified engineers to run for this position, which handles building, construction, and road projects in the county. It usually carries a full-time, four-year term.

County Treasurer: The County Treasurer usually carries an elected, four-year term, but isn't as much of a high-profile county race as Commissioner or Prosecutor.

County Prosecuting Attorney: The County Prosecutor is among the most powerful and influential elected positions you can run for on the county level. Not everyone can qualify for the seat; you need to be an attorney to run. It is usually a full-time, four-year term.

County Coroner: Surprisingly, this is actually an elected position in many counties and to run for it you usually need to have your medical license or degree. During their full-time, four-year term, County Coroners are in charge of investigating deaths in the county.

County Recorder: This is another four-year elected county office, which like County Treasurer, is a bit more low-profile. In some counties, this position is appointed, not elected.

Common Pleas Court Judge: This is another elected office that has requirements to run. In order to be a candidate, you need to have your law degree or license, and most candidates are practicing attorneys. The Court of Common Pleas in a given county usually has a General Division, Domestic Relations Division, Juvenile Division, and Probate Division. One unique thing about running in a local political campaign for Common Pleas Judge is you are not allowed to run a partisan race and cannot list on the ballot whether you are a Democrat or Republican.

Clerk of Court: You do not generally have to have a law degree to run for Clerk of Courts, but most candidates who run a political campaign for the office are attorneys. Clerk of Courts usually carries a four-year, full-time term.

Mayor: This is usually a full-time, four-year elected position, although the Mayor can also be part-time in smaller cities, villages, towns, and townships. Mayor is generally considered the most powerful local elected position in a city.

City Manager: In some cities a City Manager is elected or appointed by the city council instead of a mayor. Generally, City Managers have experience in urban planning and related fields. If the position is appointed then City Council usually launches a recruitment campaign and interviews candidates from around the state or country for the job.

City Treasurer: The City Treasurer keeps track of municipal bank accounts, income, taxes, and other money matters. It is usually a four-year term, but is not considered full-time.

City Auditor: The Auditor for a given city is also usually a four-year, part-time elected position. In most cases, successful City Auditor candidates also have similar careers and educational backgrounds.

City Law Director: This is another locally elected office that usually carries the requirement of having a law degree or license. The four-year, part-time position is in many cases held by a practicing attorney.

President of City Council: Council President is usually in charge of setting agendas, committee assignments, and chairing city council meetings. Many City Council Presidents hold office for two-year, part-time terms and are elected by the entire city.

City Ward Councilman/Alderman: City Council is in many cases made up of councilpersons who are elected in individual city wards, as well as at-large council members who are elected by the entire city. A ward councilman or councilwoman (also called Alderman and Alderwoman in some cities) only run a political campaign for office within their own ward and hold two-year, part-time terms in many cases.

At-Large Councilman: A Councilman/Councilwoman At-Large has the same duties as a ward councilperson, but they are elected by voters across the entire city instead of voters only in a specific ward.

Township/Village Trustee/Town Council: The legislative body of smaller villages, towns, and townships are usually made up of trustees, which perform duties similar to that of city councilpersons and hold two-year, part-time terms.

School Board Member/School Board President: Candidates for School Board run for elected office in the school districts where they reside and are in charge of voting on school issues. It is usually a two-year, part-time, paid position.

Precinct Committeeman, Committeewoman: Each political party in a given county (Democrats and Republicans) is usually made up of elected precinct committee members and they vote on county party issues like leadership and appointments to vacant offices. Precinct Committee members are usually elected during presidential primary elections and you can only run for precinct committeeman or committeewoman in your own precinct and for the party in which you are registered.

Alabama Governor appointed positions (not chosen by voting)
Commissioner of Insurance
Polygraph Examiners Board
Alabama Historical Commission

Alabama Indian Affairs Commission

Alabama state board of Pharmacy

Nursing Board

Alabama Board of Veterans Affairs

Medicaid Commissioner

Commissioner of department of Senior services

Director of Minority affairs

Commissioner of Department conservation and natural resources

Now that we have political foundation and we know which race we would like to step into, there are some steps for understanding what you're truly up against. Step 1: who is the opponent? Step 2: how many votes do you need to win the race? Step 3: how much is said you need vs. how much you really need to get the same result. Step 4: know the area. Sunzu said, "know thy enemy and know thyself and you need not fear a thousand battles." The following is key: remember to find out about your would-be opponent. You need their name, work history, age, community involvement, strengths, weaknesses, and major accomplishments. Know what the opponent has done and has been negligent to do. It may be beneficial for you to observe, listen, take note, and attend the opponent's functions or sessions. Remember don't give yourself away, just listen. Even if you hear things you do not agree with and goes against your moral standing, remind yourself that they will not have that position long when you stand up and run. The second step in this section is to know how many votes have been casted in every election cycle prior. Collecting this data will show you trends in voter participation and voter turnout so that you can better forecast. The turnout trends give you a ballpark figure of what it would take to be victorious on election day.

For example, comparing the participation during presidential elections versus the midterm election cycle. During the presidential election campaign season, voter's turnout is much higher. Voter enthusiasm is greater than that of a midterm election cycle because the president is not on the ballot. The third step is a very tricky one to grasp: the average cost of a particular political race. Just to forewarn you, it is usually some obscene number that only a rich person or a corporate-backed puppet can attain. The purpose of knowing that number is to understand the amount of money your opponent will be willing to spend against you. The bright side of this number is that it doesn't matter because nothing can beat the priceless effort of grassroots politics. This concept costs a lot less, but it is the option that cause, for face-to-face interactions, personal interactions, which are absolutely free and seem to be a gesture used when men have better manners. Focus on the amount needed to make a personal connection with the voters. You only need a vehicle and gas to get there and pass out business cards! The price of this token is the face-to-face interaction that will leave a lasting impression on the voters! It is literally a job interview with every hand you shake. Others spends millions on television and radio ads because they are not willing to do the legwork and they are not accustomed to defending their stance to everyday people. If you are willing to do the work, you can capitalize and gain support from thousands. For example, congressional races in the state of Alabama cost approximately $500,000.

I, Erick Wright, accomplished a well-ran and respectable campaign with less than $25,000. If you can make the personal connections and use some ingenuity with materials and social media (via Facebook Instagram and YouTube) to save money and be original. The #JustThinkWright campaign received of 50,000 votes from a large range of diverse citizens. Efforts were recognized by many in the 2nd Congressional District receiving 90% of the vote in many precincts and counties. Bullock County alone received 95% of the vote cast in favor of #JustThinkWright. During the 2014 midterm election against a millionaire incumbent, a young man with no political ties or backing was able to show how human the invincible millionaires are. We were also able to show voters that it has always been their choice, even in defeat, people could see if they did vote the outcome would be drastically different finally showing your vote really does matter!

Life after the campaign…

Montgomery to Selma

"We didn't have Nikes and all the nice shoes to wear, ah…we just had shoes" Dorothy Frazier, a marcher in Selma *1965*. I don't know, myself, I have a few pear of Nikes, boots, jackets, gloves and all that I need for travel. It doesn't cost a thing to give just your effort.

The basic concept that ideas can grow monumental if nurtured, planned, push, and executed. Ideas can spark movement, revolution, and evolution of thought. Which begs the question, "why haven't we given that effort shown by those brave heroes and heroines 1965?" I personally have given to a number of causes from antiviolence awareness, AIDS outreach, hunger relief efforts, breast cancer awareness, and drug abuse treatments. Often when participating in these different awareness groups or nonprofit organizations, fundraising is done for that entity or for that single unit. These efforts send you reminders and updates of progress. They send emails of future events; you are kept up to date and well informed on all that the organization has planned for the year. I thought to myself, being one that is given to multiple organizations, how often does the money or resources I give meet the people in need of assistance?

I devised a platform that gave everyone a chance to campaign and receive donations for their individual projects or the institutions that they recommend the most. The only stipulation of being a part of the #Strive4urcause event was effort. We would walk 54 miles from the city of Montgomery to the city of Selma. We would tell the world why we are doing this and if people feel strongly about a similar causes they can get involved with your organization or institution by donating time or material items. I committed to this challenge because I believe that the true essence of the Selma to Montgomery March and the signing of the Voting Rights Act was in part because of the people who dared to endure a treacherous 54 mile path. I have heard this story countless times growing up in Demopolis, Alabama. Selma was a close sister city so I was no stranger to the rich history and the results of our actions. I heard of men women and children that bore their own cross all the way to Montgomery, Alabama. I've heard of blistered feet of people risking their health in the rain, through muddy fields, and shoulders of U.S. Highway 80. I've heard those stories and thought to myself if I shall commit to the notion of cultural, financial, and educational uplift of my community, I, too should bear my cross the 54 miles. When making such a bold proclamation and public commit to your word, is the making of a person. A person in which you can always count to give you they're honest take on any issue.

I didn't do extreme training. Twice a week my brothers and I play basketball. In addition, my diet is very strict. I don't consume fatty foods, candies, sodas, and pork. I would like to live as long as I can, so what I consume for sustainability is very important. I stayed hydrated, drinking water as much as I can in the day. My water consumption was averaging a gallon per day.

It was announced that President Barack Obama would also be in attendance to speak to citizens that traveled from far and wide to the Selma to commemorate the 50th anniversary of Bloody Sunday and the Selma to Montgomery March. It is great whenever a sitting president visits Alabama. There was a bit of turmoil about the presidents arrival on Saturday instead of Sunday for the commemoration of the Bloody Sunday March. Local politicians and state representatives showed disgruntled opposition to the Saturday visit. It is unfortunate that when civil rights, Bloody Sunday, and the Selma to Montgomery March are used as a shot in the arm to soothe the aches of the bleeding hearts of the African American /indigenous community. These events, although symbolic, do not teach and encourage what the events are reenacted for. Our communities and political position under this order have remained unchanged, it fights against progression. Today they exploit civil rights while silencing public opinion and actively fight against anyone unwilling to continue status quo.

So my cause to walk the 54 miles was solely for that purpose of letting the indigenous population know that someone gives a damn. There were other brave souls that decided they would accept the challenge of the 54-mile-track to the historic city of Selma. On March 26 at 6:30 p.m. I saw people beginning walk the highway for what they believed in. As we went, we talked about issues and we continued to walk and finally entered into Lowndes County. Three people decided that they could not go on, so two carried on by themselves. This night was one of the most difficult things I have ever completed. If I wasn't a former collegiate football player, a four-year state track finalist, a soccer player, boxer, fencer, basketball player, and all-around athlete I would not have been able to carry on either.. This night took the cake over any training or extreme workout I have ever done.

The temperature started off as brisk, and as the miles continued, it began to drop from 60 degrees to a chilling 26 degrees. I began to feel the muscles in my legs, calves, quads, and hamstrings begin to tighten up like a ball of yarn. It made it very difficult to lift my legs or to take another step. In the back of my mind, as if auto-suggested, were the young children, elderly, men, and women who had taken this journey before. My legs churning gave my brain enough power to overlook the pain and discomfort I felt with each sharp step. I stopped once to change shoes because the terrain is not paved. There is no room from the highway to grass, mud, and debris. Incline after incline and hill after hill, my legs begin to feel like concrete. I looked at the sky, and in the night air of Lowndes County every constellation was visible. The light from the moon continues to light my path.

The company of my brethren, Adrian Ghent, helped me to regain my focus and to fight through the pain until the rally point. Ghent was participating to spread the word about community wellness and mass incarceration. We only had a tent and a few blankets to sleep outside. After receiving eight hours sleep, we rose before the sunrise and continued our journey to the historic city of Selma. The path climbed through the soft shoulder of the road, through grass, paper, and glass.

We had the discussion about building a national trail with walk way and amenities to truly receive the essence of this movement. With the help of the state, historical societies, and with the cities involved, we can create a true Freedom Trail. One that we can teach our children and others around the world about the concept of fighting for what you believe in. In the future, it is my hope that football and basketball coaches, with their players and student-athletes, can visit this trail to gain the concept of team effort. It is my goal for the future to see that newlyweds, cross country athletes, troubled youth, and others can experience such historic trail. By gaining the respect of history, we learn that change and progress must be pushed forward and fought for.

We also spoke about the upcoming festivities in Selma over the weekend. We both had mixed emotions; of excitement and eagerness for the city in the state to be shown attention an influx of customers and opportunities. When we spoke briefly about the gathering for the 50th anniversary and of the march, I expressed my emotions by simply saying, "do you think the ones that represent us saying they have the peoples best intentions at heart would be willing today to put forth the effort to walk those 54 miles to show the world what they believe in?" This question could only be answered with "no". If it only takes effort to show the people how much you care that effort would be shown a million times over. So, while we argue about the presidents arrival and who gets credit for what, the stark realities of stagnation and the decline of our communities continues.

These conversations took my mind away from the pain that I began to feel in my muscles and it made me forget about the burning and blistering of my feet. I could only thank God for brotherhood.
Adrian reminded me of this concept when he quoted an old African proverb that says, "if you want to go fast go alone, but if you want to go far, go together". And it was as true as the acres of green grass and blue skies that I saw. Because of that brotherhood and our supportive better halves, we would have surely given up. It is this unity and camaraderie we attained goodness grace.

I noticed while we traveled there were individuals, groups, churches, fraternities, sororities, and community action groups that have sponsored miles of the highway for volunteer work in order to keep the roads clean. I found this most amusing each time I passed one of the signs looked around at the debris, cotton, glass, animal carcasses, bottles, and rubber from blown-out tires. It got to the point where we were happy to see one to compare them with others and rank them on who did a better job or attempted to. The wonderful thing about having one of these signs in your name, is that you can see it at night. They have attached to them a solar light so that when the dark comes, the light is activated.

This made me wonder why in most cities in Alabama we still depend on the normal streetlights and conventional ways of light sources. It would prove smart and beneficial to place solar street lamps in more of our cities. Our current grid structure is dependent on a company or an entity's ability to provide a service for us to use. The sun is absolutely free and if we would like to capitalize on this free resource. This would be the most prudent way to replace the old street lamps and we would save the taxpayers millions every year.

Unfortunately, I'm sure there plenty companies and CEOs that would hate for this that to happen.

As we traveled down the road, we stopped for a quick respite and I changed my shoes for the third time. Laced with a new pair sneakers, a warm cup of hot chocolate, and my phone playing "Hold Own" by Dion Hawkins as a soundtrack for every step we made. As we went on, we and talked and sipped hot chocolate. I sensed something begin to happen. We saw more and more cars pass us. People began to honk their horn. Then the traffic slows down and we see flashing blue lights on the horizon. I figured it must be someone of status. I continued to walk as the motorcycle brigade passed, then came black SUVs, and some sort of a limo in the middle, followed by another SUV and more bike brigades.

We were stopped by an elderly Euro American couple, they asked if we needed a ride. I replied, "no ma'am, but thank you for the offer. We are traveling to Selma by foot." With confusion in her eye and she blushed. She asked "you guys are military, right?" They saluted us and said God bless and they drove their Prius with New York plates the next 20 miles to Selma. A white van pulled up the to side of us and a young indigenous brother asks, "did y'all walk from Montgomery?" Adrian looked him in the eye and said "yes we've been at it all day and night". The brother said "yo, yall some real niggaz". I didn't jump to rage from a person saying nigger to me. I didn't feel any form of disgrace. It is amazing to me that people still argue about someone saying this word. Even former slaves said they stripped the word of this meaning. Slaves made it their own, similar to the development of southern religion. Remember, religion was an instrument for mind control. There's stories of slave owners, hired preachers, and the "Uncle Tom" would do the preaching to the plantations. In the book "To be a Slave" by Julius Lester, he writes, "decide on your profile on the Portuguese word for black and made it nigger. It was a harsh brutal violent word that stones the soul of the slave more than the whip did his back". But the slave took this ugly word and like the white man's religion, made it their own. In their mouths it became an affectionate endearing word. He wrote, "As much was possible, they were robbed it off its ability to maim them." Mind, body, and soul intact I understood it as only our dysfunctional way of terms of endearment. To say I am a "real nigga" would be the same if I said he was a "standup guy" or "this guy is a straight shooter"; this guy is trustworthy and loyal and this guy will have my back or at least do what he said he would do.

So I showed my brother love by saying I appreciated it and left him with a positive word of endearment saying, " peace family and thanks my negus…N-E-G-U-S look it up". The brother said "thank you for standing up". He chucked the deuces and drove away.

Back to walking 10 miles to Selma and like a bolt of lightning: pain! Agonizing, excruciating, and pungent pain crashed down on me. Pain shot from my toes to my calves, my hamstrings, groin, and quad. Everything felt like it had been dipped molten lava. The terrain was getting tougher and the incline became higher and higher. Mud began to stick to our shoes and the sun was now in full glow. I needed something to take my mind away from the pain. Our mutual friends were the topic of the conversation and usually this was the most gratifying subject, for us to celebrate friends and loved ones' successes in life. We have an amazing set of friends in Ministry, Education, Busniess, , politics, NFL and Law enforcement. Sometimes when people part ways, life can have them so consumed that friendship is something easily overlook. Then Adrian tells me a quick rundown of all the people that he still keeps in contact with. we spoke about friends that's in Troy Alabama and how wonderful their families are doing. We talked about the great things our teammates are doing in Roanoke, AL and in Phoenix City, AL and Columbus, GA. We spoke about the great coaching and mentoring of our friends in Kentucky, Alabama, UAB, Smiths station, Prattville, and Elmore County. It is always great to talk about old friends and their trials in life. When speaking about these friends sometimes it can be somber. I relay to Adrian comparing it to the feeling when I lost friend and brother Rogger Webb. When my brother passed I was sad, upset, but I was at ease knowing in my heart when he lived I was the best friend or brother I could be. That gives me solace even if I never see or hear from them again.

I thought of Robert Frost , "two roads divided" and "sorry I could not take both". I wondered often about that. When I was a child and I developed an understanding of life we had the ability to make choices; those choices decided what our future would look like. The poet stood for hours and he was unsure about which road to take. Should he be safe should he take the road still with footsteps and clear breezeways or should he take the road that has fresh leaves and undergrowth? It's a simple decision of conscience, positive vs. negative, yin and yang. At the end of the day you are only left with the consequences of your actions. So do we go fast alone or far together? This is the only question in my mind when roads divide. On we walked.

"The GPS says we have 4 miles to go," said Adrian. The sun is beaming and cars are bumper to bumper filled with so many different faces. In this moment no color existed. Everyone was coming to this place which peace love in their hearts. It was said that there would be over 80,000 people in Selma to commemorate the 50th anniversary, and as from what we could see on the highway they had to be absolutely correct. Just a few miles to go our conversation were on the hometown of Adrian Ghent Madison, Florida located right outside of Tallahassee. He tells me a story about a young man in Madison Florida that fought for civil rights and voting rights for counties and cities for the indigenous population. He was apart of the NAACP while play a pivotal roles in organizational planning and effectively being the instrument of change. Ghent went on about how his home was vandalized and his family ran out of their homes because of the harassment. There was a attempted assassination but since the 60's this man still fights on the side of justice and equality to this day. Adrian said this man was named David Dukes. From what I could take from the conversation Adrian was deeply moved by the actions and the willingness to create change. David Dukes was only 17yrs old at the time of the events.

With 1 mile left and here the last stretch I feel no pain. I remember smiling, waving, stopping to take photos with drivers that had been stuck in bumper to bumper traffic for hours. Their faces would liven up. There was a glow and physical pride in people's eyes. I grabbed a stack of flyers from a group that was from Atlanta protesting against violence and mass incarceration. I walked by Southside High School, right outside of Selma, and spoke to the students and the great principle there. We even exchanged numbers and took pictures. People asked if we could take their pictures, as well as take ours. People opened the doors with smiles. People spoke to each other with pure love. I saw strangers sharing words, bottles of water, and lending a helping hand to anyone in need. This was reminiscent of the Dogon indigenous African tribe cousins; peace and harmony was the order of the day. No one was called a bitch, a whore, gay, or straight. There was no color in those moments, it was as the world should be: at ease with positive energy.

My love stood at the shoulder of the road waiting for me. I gave her a wink, a smile and said, "I'll return shortly, but I doubt if I can walk anywhere else". What a trip! What an experience! What a wonderful learning tool to fully grasp and understand what it would have been like to walk in the psyche of someone that's motivated by more than the mundane society. These people had the ability to thrive off of togetherness and onward thinking. They walked through the shallow depths, the concrete jungle. My ancestors were with me. These amazing people gained energy and motivation by positive interface. Whether singing, chanting, praying, discussing, or rejoicing until victory. Zero miles to Selma. We are here and we won't be silent.

X
The
Rise of a New Party

Mythical tales speak of a bird that rises from nothing and from ash produces the phoenix. Oh, how art often imitates life. Politically, we have been burned, used, abused, and taken advantage of. So, as we currently assess our political position, we are, but ashes, in the strong wind of destruction and political malpractice. Unfortunately, I don't hold a magic potion to make your weak political position change. There will never be a silver bullet or instant death by stake in the heart of these political vampires. Sadly, there isn't a religious doctrine that can be baptized and be politically born again. It doesn't help one person to infiltrate the system and attempt change from the inside because the system, as it stands, will corrupt the good at heart. Don't expect protection from either of the two party system, historically they have failed us each time. It has gotten so bad that representation of government, gerrymandering, access to elections and information in Alabama is similar to Iran, North Korea, and Venezuela. At this rate, Alabama will be Russia in 20 years. After the 2018 election cycle if we continue on this path ,Alabama will no longer be considered a democracy. With one party currently controlling US House of Representatives, US Senate, Supreme Court, Alabama Supreme Court, Alabama House of Representatives, and the Alabama State House, citizens of our state are now under a totalitarian rule. Throughout the course of history whenever a country leans on one rule of thought, it makes the citizens become less concerned with facts and more concern with ideology. One-sided government doesn't progress for the future, it dismantles the very fabric that makes us great. Instead of celebrating information, knowledge, diversity, science, ingenuity and art our state actively fights against it. All the while using tools to discourage advancements and competition. Some may call it the good ole boy system. I call it weak people attempting to keep others down or out.

What do I mean by this? For example, Alabama Power has monopolize the energy market in Alabama. If I gather the smartest and brightest from University of Alabama, Auburn University, and Troy to start a solar manufacturing firm, we would have to spend thousands of dollars in fake requirements, benchmarks that have nothing to do with the business, documentation for state and city, taxes for the state and city, then insurance requirements for business and if you have employees you would need workers compensation. So, it's safe to say, those very bright minds would have to embark on a 10 year journey before being able to produce the first Alabama solar panel. Ask yourself ,who does this benefit? How does this help the college graduate eager to make the world a better place and provide more jobs to community? Does it benefit homeowners and families struggling with utilities? The answers are obvious. It only benefits the rich that can afford the red tape and false requirements to do business. This process helps Alabama Power; they retain customers, allow continue price gouging, and forces the bright minds to work for them or leave the state. I'm sure that we could sit all day to discuss similar industries and the bad practices upheld by this broken system.

The issue I have with the two party system is listed as follows: one, when a party shifts so far in a direction the other party must then move to center or across the center to be relevant. A classic example is that the tea party is considered right of standard republicans. So in order for the Republican Party to capture votes, their position shifted farther right. As a result, Democrats began to change messages, advising people to not discuss health care, not to mention President Obama, never mention marijuana, or police reform. Basically, moving to a centrist or moderate republican position when democrats are said to the political left and more progressive. In Alabama everyone has been shifted to a very conservative mindset. The last mayoral race in the city of Montgomery showed how this is affecting communities. Because of lack of information (and religious conservatives ideas which run similar to tea party) a 57% black population elected and reelected an active republican that has shown repeatedly that he is uninterested in progression city wide. Because those older black conservative religious voters cast their ballots by who can quote the most bible verses, or who came to the church, or who donated to the church, and who has the most signs, that's who they vote for. Elections to these voters are a popularity contest to win the who's-who award. Never once do these voters speak about facts, read who has the best plan, they don't research, and they will not go against the church direction. At best they are trained to do as told and never question authority. The disappointing result of this is voters are politically and informationally tone deaf.

Second major issue I have with democrat and republican ideology is neither has done Alabama great justice. We are behind in every statistical category. The population is poorer, more schools are failing, and more people are being unjustly arrested for crimes that are legal in most other states. Neither political party is working towards the future and because of this life is continuing to be harder for each new generation. It's often difficult to tell someone when they are wrong, but it's more difficult to accept that you must chart a different course to correct your actions. I have personally been to democrat and republican events, just as a fly on the wall. Attending these events in hope of finding people that thought out of the box and had a vision for Alabama. What did I find? More ideology! Each time a younger person had a question or complaint, a barrage of naysayers attacked them. It's clear our opinions didn't matter to those groups when these groups need help from volunteers, young men and women they are available to help. It's unfortunate that our intellectual ability is less creditable then our physical ability to work. They use the young legs, but do not want to hear or take action on words from the young minds. This confuses me merely because millennial age groups are far more educated and current with political times, more than any other group of people.

So where do we go from here? Let's be real with ourselves. Our leadership has stated on many occasion that stepping aside or relinquishing power will only happen unless death forces it. What should we do next? Take their word as the truth? if we did this, we would get to see the kind of political representation that will acutely and effectively change this broken system. It's time to tell these party leaders if they don't change we will create the party we need.

After all, look at the tools it would have to take for a person to attempt it. One must first accept the two-party system in Alabama. Next, a person must pick a side, like religion, which is normally based on family history; not fact, figures, or intentions. Once a side has been chosen, a person must then become a part of the machine. In turn, our political identity is lost.

Malcom X said quite often, when asked about the X that follows his name, he didn't know his families name or history but he knew it wasn't 'Little'. This was such a bold statement but factual considering historic events like commodity trading and purchasing of indigenous people.

We find ourselves at the crossroads once more, not with our physical identity, but our collective political identity. We don't know what we are. Our politics were given not chosen. The terms that describes our political allegiance has yet to be invented. Our concerns and grievances will forever be a unsolved mystery. Especially if the task is given to persons that carry the title of Democrat and Republican, look for little or no progress at all.

With this political soul searching, I have found my identity my true political self. Now that I'm able to see my true identity, there are things that I can no longer accept. Consequently, there are many things that I had to accept about my political self. I now accept my history by blood and by soil. I have accepted that my natural place in this state and the planet itself. I accepted that I care more about certain topics that's hardly ever discussed in our political norm. I accepted that it will be uphill battle in a fight. I have accepted that my parents and grandparents may not understand where I'm coming from. I accepted that the millennia voters must come together as one to educate our parents and grandparents to have dialog with them and help them along the way to finding that true political self. What I no longer accept is slave laws and Django Stevens for keeping this broken system churning.

They tell us to wait, but there's money and opportunities out here. It's not like they would do what it takes to hip us to it. Well, now that I think about it, those knuckleheads probably don't know where to look. For example, President Obama may not have given black people anything, but he did leave the opportunity to do for yourself. Take the last farm bill, where billions are sitting and waiting on qualified applicants. Not only that, it was filled with programs for new and underserved farmers. Not only that, programs to mechanize and update your farm, free school and education seminars, and produce for the schools that are mandated to buy. If you are a woman, if you're black, economically disadvantaged, if you're a veteran you qualify! The cost to access these funds? No cost. A farm number is free, a tax ID number is free and a DUNS number is free, but we must do for ourselves!

Current politicians, who are mediocre at the jobs at best, don't understand or are not willing to do for themselves. If they did, Narrow Lane Rd. in Montgomery would be paved from one end to the next and not just a fresh blacktop by the country club. Also,

Fairview Ave. would be the new black Wall Street. Instead, it's a cheap rollercoaster ride with its pot-holed roads, falling infrastructure, and a forgotten history!

We have so much to do and our children will be faced with so much, so how can we wait? if we allow the same politicians to gain office : we will never have a shot at advancing education! No free head start, elementary coding classes, nor interactive learning. We will never have a shot at local ownership, land for farming, loans for banking, or retail as long as we will not do for ourselves we will never be able to create high-tech jobs in coding, microfiber, or cyber security. No green jobs such as recycling, water harvesting, solar, and renewable energy. If the current politicians understood doing for themselves we would have more locally own stores in neighborhoods instead of Dollar Generals and Family Dollar Stores. If they cared about being able to do for ourselves we would have more grocery stores, instead of package stores. We would have more banks, instead of check cashing places .Because they are not willing to do for themselves there will be no reforms in the child support system in our lifetime. There will be no reforms in the prison system. There will be no abolishment of slave taxes like the possession of marijuana. There will be no expansion of the healthcare system to support those who cannot afford to be healthy. In our time we would never see something so simple as a faster Internet. It is sad to say that in our time we would never be able to see new roads and bridges. It is pathetic that in our time we may never see a high speed train that can take a commuter from Montgomery to Huntsville to Mobile, or Birmingham to Atlanta. We will never see the prohibition of marijuana or the release of so many that are currently incarcerated by community slave tax. But yall don't hear me, you'd rather listen to goofballs, Uncle Toms, and the plain ole lost. Sorry for my brash delivery, but nobody owns me! Erick Wright ain't bought, sold, told, shushed, or ignored. I don't hope for change, we are the change!

A Man and His Thoughts; a brief summary of my viewpoints

Alabama Apartheid

I had a brief epiphany while watching the coverage of Nelson Mandela's failing health before he passed away. I thought about what this man stood for, what he spent majority of his life behind bars for and it came to me.: Nelson Mandela went up against a political structure that was made and designed to keep native born South Africans as servants for Europeans that decided to live there. It was called "Apartheid" meaning the state of being apart. They accomplish this through difference races. Blacks got the worst of everything including education, land, jobs, and hospitals. Native born Africans received a watered down education simply because learning math and science wasn't necessary to be a maid or a field hand.

At that time in history, American civil rights leaders were able to get the Civil Rights Act passed, able to get black students enrolled in University of Alabama, and abolished segregation. During that time, Alabama was one of segregation's largest supporters. Alabama also supported the restriction of the black vote by poll taxes and tests. Alabama has a rich history of voter fraud and voter oppression. The state constitution was passed based off voting fraud and the mismanagement of political office. Instead of Alabama accepting this tarnished history and work for the people that reside, there has only been the opposite.

These are all reasons why we have to learn our history. It repeats itself. Now that Mandela's health is failing and Martin Luther King is dead, who is left to stand up to these procrustean laws and draconian tactics? It is 1965 all over again! The Supreme Court recently ruled in favor of Shelby County, Alabama in striking down key components if the Voting Rights Act; the same laws that MLK gave his life to accomplish. Chief Justice John Roberts Jr. said, "our country has changed". Yes, he is correct, it has changed. You don't have white supremacy on the corner with bullhorns, chains, whips, and dogs. But what we do have is a minority rigging the game to keep themselves in power. Just like Mandela who fought against the Apartheid, that was less than 10% of the population but held 98% of power.

44

Currently in Alabama, redistricting has placed black and young civil servants out of positions. It has placed 20-year incumbents in districts with no opposition. One party controls the House and Senate, not to mention the governor's position as well. They all ran on less government intrusion and more jobs. Of the promises we've received neither good job nor less government intrusions. What we have received is the repeal of voting rights, attacks on women's right to choose, Or tax liability for foreign companies, and tax breaks for wealthy families to send children to private schools. We have also seen higher education costs increased with no addition of new jobs to pay those large student loans off. Alabamians are receiving a second rate education and no opportunity to live the American dream.

I have personally heard a foreign car manufacturer representative say, "I employee more of your people than any other company. I don't need them learning trigonometry. I need them to learn to punch divots." I was slightly taken aback, but regardless of education, these are the only decent paying jobs. Work on an assembly line, break your back with no union to back you, or leave the state. We are being treated like second-rate citizens, to go through life in servitude to the wealthiest and the politically powerful. This is not what the founders of the constitution had in mind for its citizens, it wasn't right in 1965 and it's not right now.

If you're tired of it, do more than write a letter. Let's take their jobs away and see them live on the minimum!

Why My State Should Legalize Cannabis

I believe I have come up with the most profound and logical reason why cannabis should be legal in Alabama. Wait. Before you write this off as another rant or some misinformed pot head praying for his dream to come true. I deal only in facts and logic. Where I'm from they say, "if it don't make dollars, then it don't make sense". And legalization in Alabama makes complete sense we would be insane not.

In the span of 30 years, the arrest for cannabis in the state of Alabama has quadrupled. Not only have the arrests on pot risen, but has so have the amount of violent crimes. Using this information it would be safe to say our police department has strained its resources on petty crimes, while allowing more violent perpetrators to increase our homicide rates.

Number of arrests, by drug type, 1982-2007

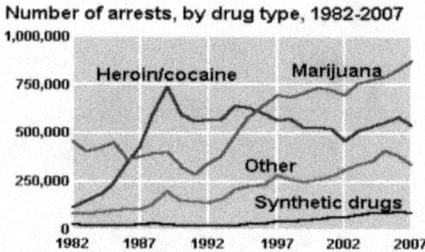

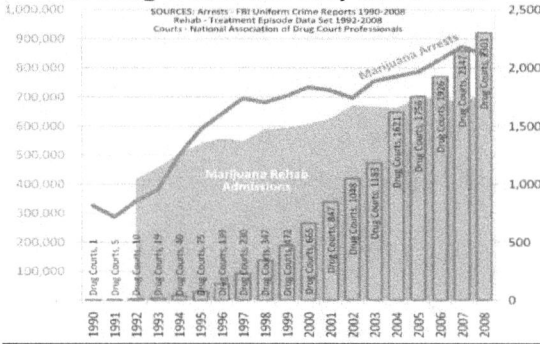

Drug Courts sentence Cannabis Consumers to Drug Treatment they don't need

SOURCES: Arrests - FBI Uniform Crime Reports 1990-2008
Rehab - Treatment Episode Data Set 1992-2008
Courts - National Association of Drug Court Professionals

Marijuana Arrests

Marijuana Rehab Admissions

Alabama is losing money! Soybean and corn crops are growing later in the year and this is causing a huge strain on farmers, the truckers that transport those goods, and the grocery stores because they have to charge more for these items. Having another crop to grow in their repertoire would be a tremendous help. We have large universities that have great agricultural departments and graduates coming out every year. Where does this talent go? You guessed it! Out of state where their talents can be appreciated. We have the richest soil surrounded by rivers; perfect for cultivation.

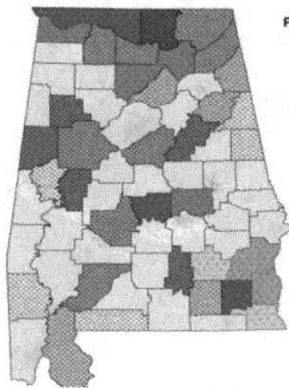

Percent Difference 2011:
NASS & DSSAT One Soil/State

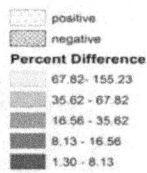

If cannabis was legalized the state would be able to capitalize on the hemp plant that Canada is currently making millions off. of Hemp can be used to make plastics, clothes, bags, and a host of other things that can be sold in Alabama markets. This creates jobs and opportunity for all. Take a look at all the things that can be developed from hemp.

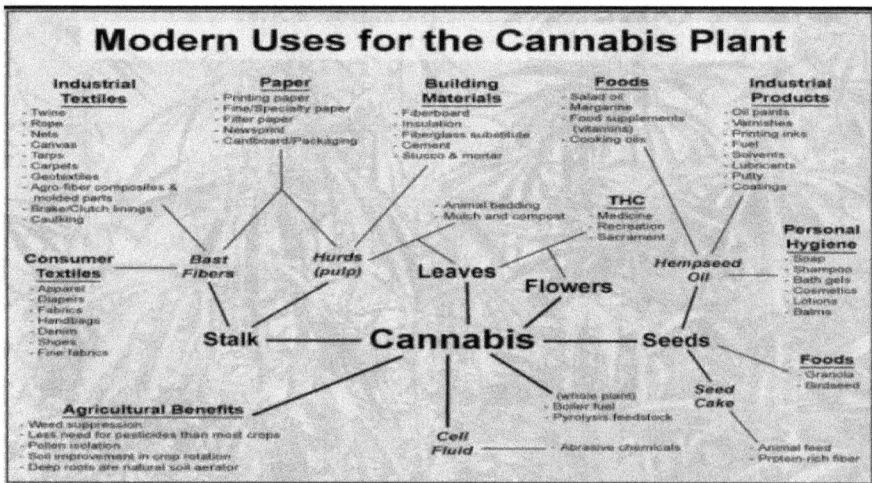

Modern Uses for the Cannabis Plant

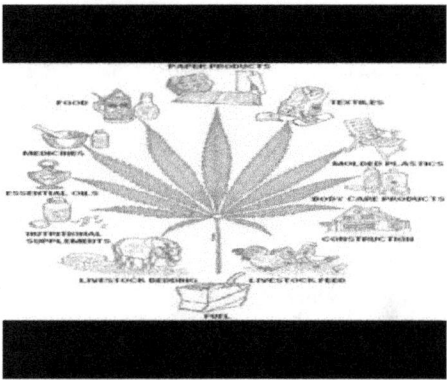

For you skeptics, I have some information for you too. Because I know the questions: how can we control it? How can we tax it? It's addictive, it's dangerous, everyone is morally against it. I HAVE GREAT NEWS !

Dependence Rates
National Institute on Drug Abuse

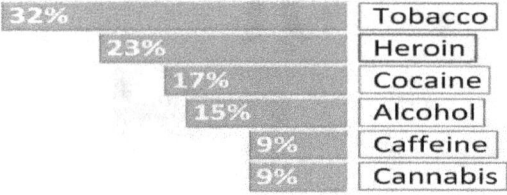

%	Substance
32%	Tobacco
23%	Heroin
17%	Cocaine
15%	Alcohol
9%	Caffeine
9%	Cannabis

Cannabis is the world's most least addictive "drug".
And, I have more great news!!!

More Today Say That Smoking Marijuana Not a Moral Issue

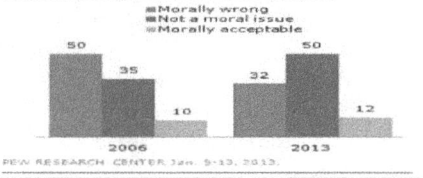

- Morally wrong
- Not a moral issue
- Morally acceptable

	2006	2013
Morally wrong	50	32
Not a moral issue	35	50
Morally acceptable	10	12

PEW RESEARCH CENTER Jan. 9-13, 2013.

No one truly cares if a person smokes weed. See the diagram below.

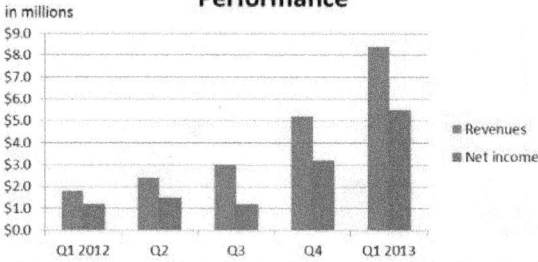

Medical Marijuana Inc.'s Financial Performance

in millions

Revenues / Net income

Q1 2012, Q2, Q3, Q4, Q1 2013

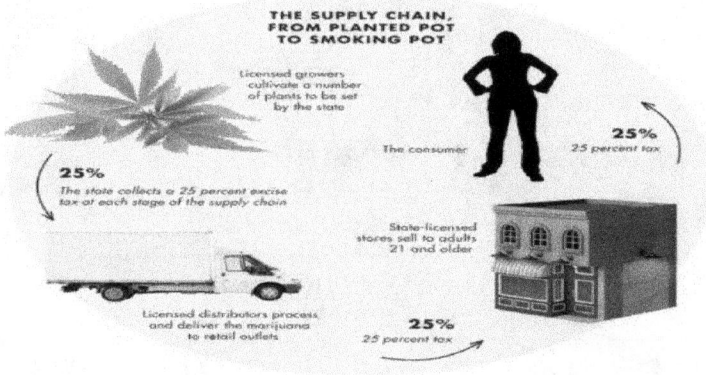

THE SUPPLY CHAIN, FROM PLANTED POT TO SMOKING POT

Licensed growers cultivate a number of plants to be set by the state

The consumer

25%
25 percent tax

25%
The state collects a 25 percent excise tax at each stage of the supply chain

State-licensed stores sell to adults 21 and older

Licensed distributors process and deliver the marijuana to retail outlets

25%
25 percent tax

This leaves, "how do we tax or control ""t. Unlike most states that don't regulate alcohol, Alabama does. We control the sales and distribution of alcohol products that aren't even made in the state. Of course we can regulate something that's home grown. Any arguments that say otherwise don't believe in the capability of our law enforcement. The state can set the tone on age, how much can be grown, and the strains. The state can also set the license amount to become a licensed grower, which is renewed yearly. This could mean hundreds of thousands of dollars for the state every year. The distribution and transportation also creates more jobs in logistics and trucking. Even the cities hoping for relief in their budgets will receive those funds.

Cities will see relief with revenue from the following:
1. Taxing the goods sold.
2. Charging for license to sale.
3. Increase sale tax revenues because of more citizens with jobs.
4. The attraction of more people moving to Alabama.

Now after looking at the facts we can ask the question: What the hell are we waiting on?

Alabama has towns where the unemployment rate has reached up to 9%. Schools are being constantly merged and teachers are being laid off; In Montgomery, homicide peaked near 30 in only six months in 2016. Farmers are going bankrupt. This is not the only way to place Alabama on the track to full legalization. Now is the time to do more than have a conversation, it's time to act! Again, what the hell are we waiting for?

When You're Young, Black, and Educated in Alabama; a creative outlook

Malcolm X, my Father; Tupac, My Big Brother

Growing up as a young, black man your faced with certain facts of life. One, for 80% of us there is no male figure in the household. Secondly, society has a preconceived notion of who we are. Three, we grow up at/or below the poverty level. Four, we get incarcerated more than any race. Five, our life span is the shortest. Six, we are most likely to die a violent death. Seven, dropout rate is the highest in the nation. Eight, we are highest diagnosed with learning disability (ADHD), and lastly, the most likely to have diabetes.

It would seem like the future would be grim for every black man, but this isn't the case. Black men are resilient, they are smart, they diligent workers, and some of the most powerful people in the world. As a whole, they could accomplish the things that history books are made out of.

When seeing the trends in society and seeing how easy it is for you to get in trouble, get pulled over, stopped and frisked, have disparity in work place and in pay, discrimination in schools and corrupt laws it hits you like a truck! The light bulb flashes on and an epiphany dawns on you!

I am that person Tupac and Malcolm X spoke about!

You could hear it in the passion of their voice. Malcolm X showed us it doesn't matter what your background was, you could still make a difference. Malcolm X gave us the example of discipline, the blueprint on direction and the proof of redemption. He died giving his last breath speaking life into us. Like a parent giving their life to protect their children. So, for this we hold him dear to us like a father. Although we have never met, he cared for me. Even though many us grow up without a dad, he left his legacy for us to pick up and carry on for the next generation.

Tupac spoke to us on the level that we understood. He did not mince word or bite his tongue and he never backed down. We saw glimpses of Malcolm X shining through Tupac. He spoke about the very things we see that plagues us. He wasn't afraid, as a black man, to walk up right. He showed that we don't have to dress a certain way to be smart. He revealed how the country will conform you into nothing more than a statistic. Like a big brother Tupac wouldn't allow us to be bullied; not by the media or by watered-down puppet rappers. He was in court monthly for reasons of nonsense, mainly because of who he was and what he stood for. He took multiple bullets to show us no matter where you, are this can be your fate. We learned many lessons watching our big brother. He gave us a real vision of America. He told us to keep our head up, steer from the bad, foster the good, and don't take any shit from nobody. "You're a Prince," he would say. He read Machiavelli's book "The Prince". He told us to cop it. We didn't know, but it's a reference to many current and former politicians. If we've learned anything from these ancestors, there is no crime in speaking your mind. We got to stand for something. Find what you're passionate about, then push! Kick it into motion! In every black man there's a scholar waiting to gather knowledge, a general ready to make plans, a creator ready to invent, and a planter waiting for some land to grow on. In every black man there's an activist waiting on his chance to speak! In every black man there's a strong father ready to teach! Shout out to our most beloved ancestors that give us the ability to spark the minds of the golden generation!

HIP HOP DONT LOVE YOU

Hip-hop, what happened to you? You used to be the reporters on the streets. Man, you used to tell us how it is as a young boy from Compton. You used to tell us about a man trying to make it out of New Orleans. Man, you used to care about us. You used be proud of your hood. You used to name every friend and every block. Man, what happened? Hip Hop you used to be the reflection of what's really going down at street level. Now what are you, Hip Hop? I don't know you at all. You're only a reflection of some shit I've never heard of or seen. I never driven one of those cars, partied days straight, popped those pills, flown in those jets, or spent a million in the club. I can't relate, but and you expect me to buy an album. You've been tamed and watered down to this form that I no longer recognize. You have people with less money than you buying into elections. Putting their own politicians in office for less than you pay for a car.

"The thinking behind it, which was very ingenious, was that state legislative races are cheap, and if you can just put a bit of money into them and flip the statehouse, then you can control the redistricting process, which in turn gives the party a great advantage in putting members of Congress in the House of Representatives," says **New Yorker** staff writer Jane Mayer.

In **North Carolina,** rich guy named Art Pope put money into 2012 election and 18 out of the 22 races his candidates won seats.

People similar to Art Pope are making cities and states change laws that continue to put us down. Our checks are getting smaller, our rights are being taken, and we continue to fill up their prisons for petty crimes that should be legal.

Hip Hop, you don't care! Did you know you could get a ticket or maybe even jail time for sagging? Did you know girls could get expelled for making dance videos? Of course you didn't. You're too busy doing your **best Sambo impression** and acting like it's all good. If you really gave a damn about us you would speak the truth regardless of who wants to hear it. If you really gave a damn you would engage in these political races, back our own people so that they can fight to adjust some of the crooked laws and unfair practices. If you really gave a damn, you would step up. How many models have you slept with? How many strip clubs have you made it rain in? How many cars and houses must you buy before you realize the truth? Hip hop is now someone's puppet. We need a hip-hop super pact. Find people that represent the culture and help them get into office. Get an agenda and lobby for your people!

My Shades of Gray

Light, but the darkness slips in. Who can be pure when the lightless creeps in? Never be defeated because pride of a million years digs in. On the side of the mountain, the ground's still loose. I have not made it from the middle, but I've climbed and climbed. All day, all night! Climbed so much 'til I can't tell day from night. Something can't be right. Pausing, maybe it's the heavy flag I've packed? That's got to be right estimation. My intentions were to boast and brag at my final destination. Surly that was my folly. No need to plant a flag when I reached the peak of the mountain.

Drops it to the ground. Soon as I released it, I began to climb higher. Noise all around me,.I see people climbing at their own pace. For saving grace, I remember days of traveling with no progress and who I climb by. Had to distance myself. Now I can climb high.

Thinking. If I keep going at this pace, I'll see the top in no time. Bright lights twinkle in my eyes. I pause and admire. Collecting gems and trophies, I stop climbing for months. After time passes by, I learn a valuable lesson that just because it shines doesn't make it a blessing.

Now I've got it! I wasn't supposed to pause at all. If the shine had a phone we shouldn't answer the call. The churning of my feet let me know I'm climbing again. Climb, Negus, climb. Till the mountain started to plateau and the guy next to me says, "this is where I'll put a small chateau". I thought he was playing 'til I noticed everyone staying. Hell, it really doesn't seem that bad. I will pause on this plateau some 'mo. I ain't there, but I ain't at the bottom. Middle class living should do for now. I spent days, nights, and years indeed, 'til I saw the plateau what satisfied the most was way too plain for my needs. My attitude for the deaf, dumb, and blind reflects it. Staying here is quite Uncle Tom-ish. When likeminded characters are so absent from my norm, I stick out like a sore thumb. Pack my bags; I must leave. It's been real, but my leg yearns for climbing fatigue. Off I go to find out that the path to the top is steeper than before. I'm reminded of Robert Frost, for I think I shouldn't ever return. But, unlike he, I gaze and the paths are many. Wishing it were only two so if one didn't work, the other shall certainly do. Many I see and I've already traveled a few. Some leading to an octagon of nowhere and others to the circle of madness where I began. I start, I stop, re-route. One step forward, then two steps back.

What a vicious cycle. I'm trying not to be devoured by this beast. I no longer desire to live this way. My ancestors won't allow me to taste defeat. So I continue the ever churning of the feet. One foot at a time one in front of the other, fighting society to just be me. All one should wish for is to be who God chose them to be. All colorful distractions are lost to me. Focus as God intended of me. Nothing shining in my eye. No plateaus to rest. No baggage to hold me back and no enemy laying siege. All I see is grey as my feet churn from night 'til day!

Nothing is by chance. It's all politics as usual. Fight the odds!

www.ingramcontent.com/pod-product-compliance
Lightning Source LLC
Chambersburg PA
CBHW060642280326
41933CB00012B/2120